Sociology of Early Palestinian Christianity

Gerd Theissen

Sociology of Early Palestinian
Christianity

Translated by John Bowden

FORTRESS PRESS
Philadelphia

Translated from the German *Soziologie der Jesus-
bewegung* ©1977 Chr. Kaiser Verlag, München.

English translation copyright ©1978 by John Bowden.

First American edition published by Fortress Press,
Philadelphia, 1978. Published under the title, *The
First Followers of Jesus,* by SCM Press Ltd., London,
1978.

Library of Congress Cataloging Publication Data

Theissen, Gerd.
    Sociology of early Palestinian Christianity.

    Translation of Soziologie der Jesusbewegung.
    Includes indexes.
    1. Sociology, Christian—Early church, ca. 30-600.
I. Title.
BR166.T4713   261.8   77-15248
ISBN 0-8006-1330-9

6518K77   Printed in the United States of America   1–1330

Contents

Abbreviations

Antt.	Josephus, *Antiquitates Judaicae*
BHT	Beiträge zur historischen Theologie, Tübingen
BJ	Josephus, *De Bello Judaico*
BZNW	Beihefte zur *Zeitschrift für die neutestamentliche Wissenschaft*, Berlin
C. Ap.	Josephus, *Contra Apionem*
CD	Damascus Document or Zadokite Document
CPJ	*Corpus Papyrorum Judaicorum*, ed. V. Tcherikover, A. Fuks and M. Stern, Cambridge, Mass. 1957ff.
ET	English translation
EvTh	*Evangelische Theologie*, Munich
GTB	Gütersloher Taschenbücher
HE	Eusebius, *Historia ecclesiastica*
IEJ	*Israel Exploration Journal*, Jerusalem
JRS	*Journal of Roman Studies*, London
JTS	*Journal of Theological Studies*, Oxford
NovTest	*Novum Testamentum*, Leiden
NTS	*New Testament Studies*, Cambridge
NZSysTR	*Neue Zeitschrift für systematische Theologie und Religionsphilosophie*, Berlin
OGIS	*Orientis Graecae Inscriptiones Selectae*, ed. W. Dittenberger, Leipzig 1903–05
PSI	*Pubblicazioni della Società Italiana, Papiri Greci e Latini*, ed. G. Vitelli, vol. VI, Florence 1920
1QM	Qumran Rule for the War, or War of the Sons of Light and the Sons of Darkness
1QS(a)	Rule of the Community or Manual of Discipline
1QpHab	Commentary on Habakkuk
SBS	Stuttgarter Bibelstudien
SVF	*Stoicorum Veterum Fragmenta*, ed. H. von Arnim, Leipzig 1921–24

TLZ	*Theologische Literaturzeitung*, Leipzig
TZ	*Theologische Zeitschrift*, Basle
WMANT	Wissenschaftliche Monographien zum Alten und Neuen Testament, Neukirchen
ZNW	*Zeitschrift für die neutestamentliche Wissenschaft*, Berlin
ZTK	*Zeitschrift für Theologie und Kirche*, Tübingen

Preface

This attempt at a sociology of the Jesus movement concludes a series of sociological studies of earliest Christianity. The work came into being while I was involved in teaching religion and German, and is addressed to readers who are also involved in practical work of this kind. I have developed some of the arguments presented here at more length in learned journals, and anyone interested may pursue them there.

I am grateful to numerous professional colleagues who have encouraged my sociological researches into the New Testament, whether by criticism or by approval. Pride of place must go to my revered teacher Philipp Vielhauer. I am grateful to the editors of the series for accepting my study for Theologische Existenz heute, and to all the staff and workers of the publishers and printers, known to me and unknown, for their care and effort. Above all, I am grateful to my wife: that I am able to pursue my theological work with such freedom and peace of mind is largely due to her. Without this independence I could never have written this book. In dedicating it to my wife, I do so for what she has done, and not because she is one of the family.

Bonn, February 1977

For Christa

1. Aims and Methods of a Sociology of the Jesus Movement

1. The Jesus movement

Earliest Christianity began as a renewal movement within Judaism brought into being through Jesus. The transitions to the first Hellenistic Christianity and to Jewish Christianity are not clearly marked. Geographical and chronological data give us a rough and ready means of demarcation: the first Hellenistic Christianity developed predominantly outside Palestine, whereas the Jesus movement was a Palestinian phenomenon which spilled over into the neighbouring regions of Syria. It became a particular form of Christianity, Jewish Christianity, after AD 70. Before that it had been in competition with other renewal movements within Judaism; afterwards, Pharisaism gained the upper hand in Judaism, and the Christians were excommunicated. Thus the Jesus movement is the renewal movement within Judaism brought into being through Jesus and existing in the area of Syria and Palestine between about AD 30 and AD 70.

2. The aims of a sociology of the Jesus movement

The aim of a sociology of the Jesus movement is to describe typical social attitudes and behaviour within the Jesus movement and to analyse its interaction with Jewish society in Palestine generally.[1] A distinction must be made between the analysis of roles, of factors and of function. An analysis of roles investigates typical patterns of behaviour; an analysis of factors the way in which this behaviour is determined by society; an analysis of function its effects upon society. No attempt is made to find a social 'first cause', as economic, ecological, political and cultural factors cannot be separated in their reciprocal interaction. In the same way, it is unnecessary to give a univocal definition of the function of religion, since this can contribute in a variety of ways towards fulfilling the basic aims of a society, namely in achieving the integration of its members and overcoming conflicts through change. Integration can involve compulsion and restrictions, but it can also mean the extension and the enrichment of human possibilities. Conflicts can either be suppressed by compensatory solutions or brought to a head by new plans for their resolution. Religion has at least four possible functions, which can be set out in the following pattern: [2]

	Integrating function	Antagonistic function
Restrictive function	*Domestication* Internalized social pressure	*Compensation* Illusory resolution of conflicts
Creative function	*Personalization* Socialization of natural human qualities	*Innovation* Realization of potential for conflict, new resolutions

Religion can be a social cement and an impulse towards renewal: it can intimidate people and force them to conform, or it can help them to act independently. All these functions can also be noted in primitive Christianity. However, it is unmistakable that the innovative function of religion appears more clearly here than almost anywhere else.

3. The methods of a sociology of the Jesus movement

Whether or not it is possible to make a sociological study of the Jesus movement depends on the sources and the relevant source material which they contain. Unfortunately, this source material is scanty and difficult to use; there are disputes over the way in which it should be interpreted and it can hardly be said to have had an interest in communicating data for sociology. Thus all sociological information has to be extracted laboriously by a process of inference. Three different procedures may be distinguished here: [3]

(*a*) *Constructive conclusions* are drawn from an evaluation of pre-scientific statements which give either prosopographic information about the origin, property and status of individuals or sociographic information about the programme, organization and patterns of behaviour of whole groups.

(b) *Analytical conclusions* are drawn from texts which afford an indirect approach to sociological information. Statements about recurring events, conflicts between groups or over ethical and legal norms, literary forms and poetic modes of expression (e.g. parables) are all illuminating in this respect.

(*c*) *Comparative conclusions* are drawn from analogous movements to be found in the world of the time. The more widespread a pattern of behaviour was in Palestinian Jewish society, the more we may assume that it was socially conditioned. We must therefore pay special attention to the other renewal movements within Jewish society which can be found alongside the Jesus movement, that is, the Essenes and the Zealots.

The remarks which follow will indicate whether the sources provide sufficient data to justify an attempt at a sociology of the Jesus movement. Scepticism on grounds of methodology is understandable and legitimate. We know very little. Much must remain conjectural. Nevertheless, scientific work is legitimate as long as better and worse hypotheses can be weighed against one another.

4. The sources

The synoptic gospels are the most important sources for the Jesus movement; the historical works of Josephus the most illuminating sources for the Jewish world of the time. In the case of the synoptic gospels we have to remove material which is of Hellenistic origin. We can make use of all the rest. Thus we may leave open the question whether the traditions about Jesus are true or false. If we presuppose that a tradition is genuine, we may assume that those who handed it down shaped their lives in accordance with the tradition. If we assume that it originated

within the Jesus movement in the period after Easter, we can
presuppose that those who handed it down shaped the tradition
in accordance with their life. In either case the result is the same:
there is a correspondence between the social groups which
handed down the tradition and the tradition itself. Thus a
sociology of the Jesus movement transcends the dispute of both
'conservative' and 'critical' exegetes over the authenticity and
historicity of the tradition. It is unaffected by the dilemmas of the
quest for the historical Jesus. Indeed, it does make a contribution towards solving these problems. For it suggests that we
should assume a continuity between Jesus and the Jesus
movement and in so doing opens up the possibility of transferring
insights into the Jesus movement to Jesus himself.[4]

5. Preliminary comments on a sociological analysis of earliest Christianity

Objections are often made more to the legitimacy of a sociological
study of Christianity than to the feasibility of carrying it out; it is
said to start from a one-sided view of its subject and to stand in
the way of 'true' understanding. It is objected, for example, that
sociology covers only general patterns, and leaves the individual
out of account. Certainly, it is true that a sociology of the Jesus
movement is confined to its more general, structural aspects. But
it is well aware of this limitation. It does not claim to do justice to
every aspect of the subject. Quite apart from this, the more
clearly the general background can be established, the more
clearly individual elements stand out from what is universal and
typical. Jacob Burckhardt's words should, however, be a warning
against underestimating the importance of the universal and the
typical: 'On average, generalized facts, like those of cultural history, may prove more important than particular facts; happenings
which recur may be more important than those which are
unique.'[5] And who could accuse Burckhardt of being deficient in an
understanding of the importance of the individual?

A further objection is that sociology reduces religious phenomena to non-religious factors. Now it is true that sociology
establishes more connections between religious and non-religious

phenomena than those who adopt a specifically religious stand-point would accept. However, a one-sided causal derivation of religious phenomena from social facts is only one possible inter-pretation of these connections, and it is an improbable one at that. Usually it is more satisfactory to assume an interaction between the two. Moreover, we must make a strict distinction between origin and validity, avoiding the genetic fallacy. The validity of an idea is quite independent of whatever causes may have given rise to it in the first place.

These are only two objections to sociological investigation of the earliest Christianity. Further deep and dark suspicions on principle, following similar lines, are also cherished. However, we need not go into them here. For on principle, the burden of proof does not lie with those who raise questions, but with those who reject them as being inadmissible. We may therefore content ourselves with a few preliminary remarks in defence of a sociology of the Jesus movement. People are generally curious about circumstances which are veiled in an aura of piety; this aura makes it difficult for many to get to the heart of the matter. We are, moreover, obliged to arrive at the best possible assessment of the decisive events in our history. This presupposes the know-ledge of historical and social conditions. Then, finally, in studying the Jesus movement we come up against a central question con-cerning the life of man in society: in situations of social tension, how is renewal possible without giving rein to the destructive aggression which renewal brings about? In my view these con-cerns are legitimate, and the best basis on which they can be pursued is to be prepared to correct prejudices, to be sympathetic to the matter under consideration, and to remember that there are two sides to everything.

Part One

Analysis of Roles: Typical Social Attitudes in the Jesus Movement

The internal structure of the Jesus movement was determined by the interaction of three roles: the wandering charismatics, their sympathizers in the local communities, and the bearer of revelation. There was a complementary relationship between the wandering charismatics and the local communities: wandering charismatics were the decisive spiritual authorities in the local communities, and local communities were the indispensable social and material basis for the wandering charismatics. Both owed their existence and legitimation to their relationship to the transcendent bearer of revelation. Their relationship to him was characterized by reciprocal expectations. The various christologies express the attitudes of expectation directed towards the bearer of revelation, the ethical and religious commandments formulate what he expected of believers. Mutually determined roles are assigned to both.[6]

II. The Role of the Wandering Charismatics

The first argument that we need to test against the sources is that Jesus did not primarily found local communities, but called into being a movement of wandering charismatics. The decisive figures in early Christianity were travelling apostles, prophets and disciples who moved from place to place and could rely on small groups of sympathizers in these places. From the point of view of organization, these groups of sympathizers remained within the framework of Judaism. They were less obviously the embodiment of the new element which had emerged with earliest Christianity, and a variety of obligations and ties entangled them in the old situation. It was, rather, the homeless wandering charismatics who handed on what was later to take independent form as Christianity. Use of the term 'charismatic' keeps in view the fact that their role was not an institutionalized form of life, a position which someone could adopt as a result of his own decision. The role of the charismatic is grounded in a call over which he had no control. As we shall demonstrate in the sections which follow, by means of the process of argument indicated briefly above, this role gave form to the Jesus movement.

1. Constructive conclusions

According to Luke, the earliest community in Jerusalem was governed by twelve apostles (Acts 1.12ff.). Here Luke projects into the past his ideal of a local community with collegiate government. It is a projection, for when Paul visited Jerusalem three years after his conversion, Peter was the only member of this supposed church leadership whom he found there (Gal. 1.18). Where were the others? The most likely explanation is that they were travelling through the country, on a mission of preaching and healing. This is the commission they had been given in Mark 3.13: nothing had been said about governing a community. Fifteen years later Paul met only 'three pillars' in Jerusalem, among them Peter (Gal. 2.9), who was often on journeys (Acts 8.14; 9.32ff.; 10.1ff.; Gal. 2.11ff.; I Cor. 1.12). The group of twelve under his leadership soon disappeared. According to Matt. 19.28 its task lay among the twelve (scattered) tribes of Israel. The group probably dispersed to all points of the compass. The same is true of the group around Stephen. Allegedly chosen to relieve the twelve of work in the distribution of provisions and at the same time to give due care to Hellenistic members of the community, its members soon emerged as independent missionaries (Acts 8.4; 11.19ff.). Their mobility is not just to be dated after their expulsion from Jerusalem. One of them came from Antioch (Acts 6.5). There was a group of five there composed of men from all over the world (Acts 13.1): Barnabas came from Cyprus (Acts 4.36), Paul from Tarsus (Acts 22.3), Lucius from Cyrenaica; Menahem was brought up with Prince Herod Antipas – either in Jerusalem or in Rome. Paul and Barnabas were travelling preachers. We may assume that this is also true of the others. In principle they too would be involved in the mission for which Paul and Barnabas were 'set apart' (Acts 13.2). Thus Antioch was the 'home' of a group of wandering charismatics. However, strange wandering charismatics also appeared here, including the prophet Agabus (Acts 11.27ff.) who also travelled through Judaea and Caesarea (Acts 21.10). Wandering prophets and teachers were still the decisive authorities at the time of the Didache (in the first half of the second century); they would settle for a period in a particular community (Didache 13.1f.). Their superiors were still the 'apostles', who lived 'in accordance with the teaching of the gospel' and were allowed to stay no more than three days in one place (11.3ff.). All these wandering charismatics had a higher reputation than local ministers (15.2). No wonder that this reputation was misused. The Didache gives a warning against travelling Christian prophets who peddled Christ (12.5). The satirist Lucian made one of these prophets the butt of his satire and denigrated him as a parasitical vagabond – probably unjustly (*Peregrinus* 16). He was certainly not the only one to have such a low opinion of these figures. We meet their successors once again in the Pseudo-Clementine *Epistulae ad virgines*. Elsewhere too, all down the ages, countless others have renounced the idea of a home for the wandering life of an apostle. We may assert that what information we have about the first early Christian authorities points to wandering charismatics.

2. Analytical conclusions

Wandering charismatics were not a marginal phenomenon in the Jesus movement. They shaped the earliest traditions and provide the social background for a good deal of the synoptic tradition, especially the tradition of the words of Jesus. Much here that at first sight seems strange and eccentric becomes more comprehensible when we remember those who handed down these sayings and put them into practice. The most illuminating feature here is that of the ethical norms, since they relate directly to the attitudes of Jesus' followers, in particular the pattern of giving up home, family, possessions and protection, which we find in this connection.

(i) *Homelessness*   Giving up a fixed abode was an essential part of discipleship. Those who were called left hearth and home (Mark 1.16; 10.28ff.), followed Jesus, and like him became homeless. 'Foxes have holes, and birds of the air have nests; but the Son of man has nowhere to lay his head' (Matt. 8.20) is a saying which applied to them. Now one might suppose that after the death of Jesus the disciples returned to a settled life. But quite apart from the practical difficulties – once someone had left his home town he would find it hard to put down roots again there – we hear nothing to this effect. We only hear that some remained in Jerusalem (and therefore left their home country of Galilee); we may assume that most continued their life of wandering, 'the behaviour of the Lord', as the Didache puts it (11.8). The discourse at the sending out of the twelve (Matt. 10.5ff.) enjoins a wandering life upon them, and the Didache makes the unequivocal judgment: 'An apostle who remains more than two days is a false prophet' (11.5). It is obvious that this homelessness was not always simply a matter of choice. Matthew 10.23 is an obvious reference to the persecution of wandering charismatics: 'When they persecute you in one town, flee to the next; for truly, I say to you, you will not have gone through all the towns of Israel before the Son of man comes.' They were persecuted (cf. Matt. 23.34; Acts 8.1) and rejected in many places (Matt. 10.44).

(ii) *Lack of family* One marked feature of the wandering Christian charismatics is their lack of family: they had left this behind, along with their hearth and home (Mark 10.29). The break with their family included disregard for the demands of piety: one disciple was forbidden to bury his dead father (Matt. 8.22). Others abandoned their fathers at work (Mark 1.20). Indeed, hatred of all members of the family could be made a duty:

> If any one comes to me
> and does not hate his own father and mother
> and wife and children
> and brothers and sisters,
> yes, and even his own life,
> he cannot be my disciple (Luke 14.26).

The saying in praise of castration (Matt. 19.10f.) also indicates a disregard for family. We can understand why the earliest Christian prophet did not have much of a reputation in his ancestral city, where the forsaken families still lived (Mark 6.4). Perhaps Peter acquired his surname 'bar Jonah' in this connection (Matt. 16.17). In John 1.42 it is rendered 'son of John', but bar Jonah would mean 'son of Jonah'. In my view it is worth considering the interpretation which derives bar Jonah from 'wild, empty, desolate', and understands the surname in the sense of 'outlaw', 'outcast'. In the eyes of those whom he had abandoned, Peter was probably a 'bar Jonah', someone who lived in the wilderness and led the life of an outsider on the fringe of society.

Probably many families had the same feelings about their sons who had joined the Jesus movement as did the family of Jesus about their 'lost son': they simply thought that he was mad (Mark 3.21). In the discourse connected with the sending out of the twelve this judgment is expressly made into a generalization: 'A disciple is not above his teacher nor a slave above his master. If they have called the master of the house Beelzebul, how much more will they malign those of his household' (Matt. 10.24f.). Of course the members of the Jesus movement defended themselves against the charge of having a completely negative attitude towards the family. In part they justified their position by reshaping the concept of the family: true kindred were not those born into the family but those who heard and did the word of God (Luke 8.19–21). Praise was accorded, not to the mother of Jesus but to those who heard his words (Luke 11.28ff.). The disciples found a hundredfold recompense for the families they had left behind in those who sympathized with the Jesus movement: 'houses and brothers and sisters and mothers and children and fields' – even in this age (Mark 10.30). The tradition says nothing about the way in which the families who have been abandoned are to find a substitute for the earning power which they have lost, but it does not conceal the unavoidable differences between the followers of Jesus and their families. There was consolation in the thought that this sort of thing was part of the tribulations of the last days and therefore was a necessity (Luke 12.52f.; Matt. 10.20).

(iii) *Lack of possessions* A third characteristic of the earliest Christian wandering charismatics was their criticism of riches and possessions. Someone who was manifestly poor, without money, shoes, staff or provisions, and with only one garment, who travelled the roads of Palestine and Syria (Matt. 10.10), could criticize riches and the possession of property without losing credibility. This was especially true if he had given away his own possessions. This was the mark of complete discipleship. It is why the rich young man could not commit himself to it (Mark 10.17ff.). Barnabas was a man of a different stamp: he sold part of his possessions (Acts 4.36f.). Anyone who acted in this way could put forward the view that it was easier for a camel to go through the eye of a needle than for a rich man to enter the kingdom of God (Mark 10.25), and he could advise men to lay up treasure in heaven and not on earth (Matt. 6.19ff.). He could warn men that they could not serve both God and mammon (Luke 16.8), and threaten that the imminent crisis in the world would overturn all earthly relationships:

> Woe to you that are rich, for you have received your consolation.
> Woe to you that are full now, for you shall hunger.
> Woe to you that laugh now, for you shall mourn and weep
> (Luke 6.24f.).

To work off their aggression, in vivid imaginary pictures they depicted the fearful end of the rich and the good fortune of the poor in the world to come (Luke 16.19–31). This is the way that the deprived have always consoled themselves. Here, however, there was more to it than that. Here poverty was not only a fate, but a calling. For the wandering charismatics were not allowed more than the most basic day's ration. This was what 'the ordinance of the gospel' required (Didache 11.3ff.). This manifest poverty was based on an unconditional trust in the goodness of God, who would not let his missionary come to grief:

> Therefore I tell you, do not be anxious about your life, what you shall eat or what you shall drink, nor about your body, what you shall put on. Is not life more than food, and the body more than clothing? Look at the birds of the air: they neither sow nor reap nor gather into barns, and yet your heavenly Father feeds them. Are you not of more value than they?...(Matt. 6.25–32).

It is wrong to read words like this in the mood of a family walk on a Sunday afternoon. There is nothing here about delight in birds and flowers and green fields. On the contrary, these words express the harshness of the free existence of the wandering charismatics, without homes and without protection, travelling through the country with no possessions and no occupation. The final words, 'Therefore do not be anxious about tomorrow, for tomorrow will be anxious for itself. Let the day's own trouble be sufficient for the day' (Matt. 6.34), may well be born of bitter experience. Wisdom of this kind, expressed by travelling charismatics, is quite as credible as the prayer for daily bread, i.e. for the day's ration. These people depended on the haphazard support of sympathizers, to whom they could offer preaching and healings as recompense (Luke 10.5ff.); and seen from outside that did not amount to much. Preaching consisted of words, and healings did not happen every day, so that settled sympathizers had to be given a special motivation if they were to support the wandering charismatics: 'Whoever gives to one of these little ones a cup of cold water because he is a disciple, truly, I say to you, he shall not lose his reward' (Matt. 10.42). To put it plainly: to begin with, support was no more than bread cast on the waters. Only in the future judgment would its usefulness be shown. At that time a welcome to apostles and prophets would provide magical protection, and rejection of them would exact its revenge (Luke 10.5ff.). This may not have been normal begging, but it was begging indeed: begging of a high order, charismatic begging, based on the confidence that the problem of finding enough to live on would be solved on the principle: 'Seek...first the kingdom of God and his righteousness, and all these things shall be yours as well' (Matt. 6.33).

(iv) *Lack of protection*   To relinquish all rights and all protection was a deliberate risk. Anyone who walked along ancient roads without a staff made it clear that he had absolutely nothing to defend himself with. This was the relevant situation for the command not to resist evil, to offer the left cheek if one is struck on the right (Matt. 5.38f.). The admonition to go two miles with anyone who asks you to go one (Matt. 5.41) would be of immediate relevance to the situation of a wandering charismatic. It will not matter to anyone who is travelling anyway whether he is pressed into service for one mile or for two. This refusal to offer any defence was also maintained before the authorities and in courts. The charismatics left it to the Holy Spirit to find the right words (Matt. 10.17ff.).

3. A comparative conclusion

The wandering Cynic philosophers are in some way analogous to the earliest Christian wandering charismatics. They too seem to have led a vagabond existence and also to have renounced home, families and possessions. In his remarks about the Cynics, Epictetus asks how it is possible to live a happy life without goods and possessions, naked, without hearth or home, without anyone to care, without a slave, without a homeland. He continues:

> Look, God has sent you someone who can prove to you as a matter of fact that this is possible. I have none of that. I lie on the bare earth; I have no wife, no children, no little mansion – only earth and heaven and one large cloak. Yet what do I lack? Am I not free from cares, without fear? Am I not free? (*Diss.* III. 22.46–48).

These outsiders too were persecuted, for instance under Vespasian (Suetonius, *Vespasian* 10). Their affinity to the early Christians is also demonstrated by the way in which the early Christian wandering charismatic Peregrinus could be converted to Cynicism. True, these analogies take us outside Palestine, but from an early stage the influence of the Jesus movement extended more widely. Wandering charismatics appeared in Antioch (Acts 13.1ff.) and among the Pauline communities where, as in Corinth, they made difficulties for Paul.

4. Summary

The ethical radicalism of the synoptic tradition is connected with this pattern of wandering, which could be carried on only under extreme and marginal conditions. Such an ethos could only be practised and handed down with any degree of credibility by those who had been released from the everyday ties of the world, who had left hearth and home, wife and children, who had let the dead bury their dead, and who took the lilies and the birds as their model. It only had a chance in a movement of outsiders. No wonder that we keep meeting outsiders in the tradition: the sick and the crippled, prostitutes and good-for-nothings, tax collectors and prodigal sons. The vivid eschatological expectations of these early Christian wandering charismatics went along with their role as outsiders: they lived as those who expected the end of the world. The more they detached themselves from this world in their everyday actions, the more they kept destroying this world in their mythical fantasies, as if they had to work off their rejection by this world. How natural it was to consign hostile places to the fire and flames of the last judgment (Luke 10.14f.)! Granted, they fought against such visions of vengeance (Luke 9.51ff.), but this only confirmed their existence.

III. The Role of Sympathizers in the Local Communities

It is impossible to understand the Jesus movement and the synoptic tradition exclusively in terms of the wandering charismatics. In addition to them there were 'local communities', settled groups of sympathizers. The term 'community' may be misleading. For these groups remained wholly within the framework of Judaism and had no intention of founding a new 'church'. Unfortunately we know very little about them.

1. Constructive conclusions

Jesus himself found a welcome in the homes of sympathizers, e.g. with Peter (Matt. 8.14), Mary and Martha (Luke 10.38ff.), Simon the leper (Mark 14.3ff.); some women gave him material support (Luke 8.2f.). Such sympathetic families were probably the nucleus of later local communities. We have no more information than that. The only local communities in Palestine of which we have knowledge are in Jerusalem (Acts 1ff.) and Judaea (Gal. 1.22). They were more numerous in the Hellenistic city-states, in Caesarea (Acts 10.1ff.), Ptolemais (21.7), Tyre and Sidon (21.3f.), Antioch (11.20ff.) and Damascus (9.10). Perhaps we might conclude from an argument from silence that they were less important in Palestine than in the Hellenistic world. In Palestine, only the Jerusalem community attains any prominence. It may have been the home community for the first Christian wandering charismatics (say for Peter and Agabus). Soon, however, James the brother of the Lord had the chief say in it, and he was no wandering charismatic (cf. Acts 12.17; 15.13; 21.18; Josephus, *Antt.* 20.9.1, §200; Eusebius, *HE* II. 23.4ff.).

2. Analytical conclusions

There are very few synoptic traditions the unmistakable setting of which is the life of local communities. They include the synoptic apocalypse, which calls for men to leave their homes at the time of the final catastrophe (Mark 13.14ff.). At a stroke, the text sheds light on the mentality of the local communities. Even here there was a latent readiness to leave home; here too people entertained the possibility that soon they would become homeless fugitives. The example of the wandering charismatics may have reinforced this readiness. In general, however, the local communities were less radical than the wandering charismatics. This is shown in the case of three problems which every group had to solve in some way: regulations for behaviour, the structure of authority and the procedure for accepting and rejecting members.

(i) *Regulations for behaviour*   Among the local communities, various influences had a marked effect on norms of behaviour. The limiting factors of profession, family and neighbours all played a part. It was impossible to act as freely towards the law as did the wandering preachers who had no ties. When we find radical and more moderate norms in the gospels side by side, it would seem obvious to connect this juxtaposition with the close association of wandering charismatics with local communities, even if it is never possible to assign the various sayings clearly to one or other social form of the Jesus movement: the traditions of the wandering charismatics were obviously known in the local communities (and vice versa). Some communities wanted to see the law fulfilled down to the smallest detail (Matt. 5.17ff.) instead of criticizing it (Matt. 5.21ff.). They felt that scribes and Pharisees were legitimate authorities (Matt. 23.1ff.) instead of morally corrupt groups over which one could only throw up one's hands in horror (Matt. 23.13ff.). They recognized the temple and its priesthood through sacrifice (Matt. 5.23), paying the temple tax (Matt. 17.24ff.) and accepting priestly declarations of wholeness (Mark

1.44), instead of rejecting its cultic practices (Mark 11.15ff.). They accepted patterns of fasting practised around them (Matt. 6.16f.) and had a positive attitude towards marriage and the family (Mark 10.2ff.; 10.13ff.). In some respects they deliberately practised outward conformity, while retaining inward reservations. For they were aware that in fact they had been released from the temple tax (Matt. 17.26) and that the declaration of wholeness by the priest was really superfluous (Mark 1.44); in the last resort, scribes and Pharisees were questionably authorities, whose words did not correspond with their actions (Matt. 23.3). In the end, reconciliation was more important than sacrifice (Matt. 5.23). They knew that in giving alms, praying or fasting, what mattered was not the externals, but the inner motive, which was manifest only to God (Matt. 6.1ff.). These rules for religious practice are illuminating in themselves; in my view they can clearly be located in local communities. Only there could one find a quiet 'room' (Matt. 6.6), only there was there social pressure from neighbours and public opinion which people sought to escape by hiding away.[7] At this point it was necessary to stress a concern to fulfil the laws, the customs and the norms of society – possibly even more completely than in the world around; this was the context for the search for the 'better righteousness' (Matt. 5.20).

Thus there was a gradated series of norms for wandering charismatics and local sympathizers. We also have direct evidence for this. In Matthew, the rich young man is first of all asked to observe all the commandments. Only after this is he summoned to become a disciple. His call is put in conditional, rather than apodeictic, terms: 'If you would be perfect, go, sell what you possess and give to the poor . . .' (Matt. 19.21). There are special rules for those who are perfect. The Didache puts it in a similar way: 'If you can bear the whole yoke of the Lord, you will be perfect, but if you cannot, do what you can' (Didache 6.2).

(ii) *The structure of authority* At first, wandering charismatics were the authorities in the local communities. In any case, local authorities were unnecessary in small communities. Where two or three were gathered together in the name of Jesus (Matt. 18.20), a hierarchy was superfluous. Problems were resolved either by the community as a whole or by wandering charismatics who happened to arrive. Thus we find juxtaposed sayings which assign the authority to bind and to loose on the one hand to the community and on the other to Peter (a wandering charismatic) (Matt. 18.18; 16.19). We may compare the contradiction between rejecting all authority (Matt. 23.8ff.) and recognizing early Christian 'prophets, wise men and scribes' (Matt. 23.34). This contradiction is easy to understand. The less the structures of authority in local communities had come under the control of an institution, the greater was the longing for the great charismatic authorities. And conversely, the greater the claim of these charismatics to authority, the less interest there was in setting up competing authorities within the communities. But when the local communities grew in size, there was a need for internal government which inevitably competed with the wandering preachers. This is probably the explanation of the differences between Peter and James. Peter, a wandering charismatic with no ties, was more in a position to risk coming into conflict with Jewish food regulations than James, the spokesmen for the community in Jerusalem. Peter ate with Gentile Christians in Antioch, but James sent emissaries to make him conform with Jewish norms (Gal. 2.11f.). The same sort of thing happens in the second century: the wandering charismatic Peregrinus ate something that was forbidden, was criticized by the local communities and lost his influence with them (Lucian, *Peregrinus* 16). The Didache shows that conflicts of this kind did not simply go back to personal animosities. Here the bishops and deacons elected by the local communities are clearly subordinated to the elect travelling charismatics. It is necessary for an explicit warning to be given: 'Do not despise them, for they are your honourable men together with the prophets and teachers' (15.2). Prophets and teachers, on the other hand, including wandering charismatics, are to be received as the Lord (11.2). They have to be fed (11.6; 13.1ff.). They have the same privileges as the Old Testament priesthood (13.3; cf. I Cor. 9.13f.), indeed, they are even given precedence over the poor (13.4; cf. Mark 14.7). At the same time, however, this obligation to support the wandering charismatics made the communities critical: prophets who show all too clear an interest in money and food are to be rejected as false prophets (11.9, 12). A couple of steps further and we are in the position of Diotrephes in III John, who forbade all support of whatever kind for wandering charismatics. But that happened in the late New Testament period. During the time of the Jesus movement the sway of the wandering charismatics was maintained unbroken.

(iii) *The procedure for accepting and rejecting members* Membership of the community had to be determined by the local community itself. Baptism, originally an eschatological sacrament, intended as protection against the coming judgment and as a sign of conversion, probably became the decisive rite of initiation in the local communities (Matt. 28.19; Didache 7). There are no instructions for administering baptism in the commission given to the wandering charismatics (the only exception is Matt. 28.19). Paul expressly states that baptism is not one of his tasks (I Cor. 1.17). It had no significance for the life of the wandering charismatic. Anyone who has left his hearth and home has clearly bidden farewell to the world. The call to discipleship made any rite of initiation superfluous. But this call was unpredictable, and baptism could be institutionalized. Regulations also emerged in the local communities for the exclusion of 'sinners'. Three procedures are provided for in Matt. 18.15ff.: personal warning, a conversation in the presence of two witnesses, and expulsion from the assembly of the community. There were similar rules in Qumran (1QS 5.26f.). We do not hear of any rules for excluding wandering charismatics. According to Didache 11.1 they were subject to the judgment of God. Special precautions were unnecessary. If they ceased to visit their communities, they lost their basis for support (cf. Lucian, *Peregrinus* 16).

3. A comparative conclusion

We have an analogy in contemporary Judaism to the juxtaposition of radical and moderate demands. Among the Essenes there were groups with a very strict ethos, renouncing both possessions and marriage (*BJ* 2.8.2–12, §§119ff.; cf. 1QS 6.19), and also groups with a more temperate ethos, in which both marriage (*BJ* 2.8.13, §§160f.; CD 7.6f.) and possessions (CD 13.14; 14.13) were tolerated. We may assume that the stricter group was centred in Qumran, since it would have been easier to put the more radical pattern into effect in an oasis in the desert than in the midst of society. The more temperate ethos will have been represented by groups which lived scattered about (*BJ* 2.8.4, §§124ff.) in 'camps' (CD 7.6f.). There was lively communication between all groups. In every city someone was entrusted with responsibility for looking after all members travelling through, 'to provide them with clothing and to see to all other needs' (*BJ* 2.8.4, §125). True, these travelling Essenes were not wandering charismatics (we have no exact information on the matter), but the hospitality of Essene groups is very similar to the hospitality of local Christian communities towards their wandering preachers. We also find the same gradations of membership. At the same time, there are unmistakable differences. And they are very important from a sociological point of view. The local Christian communities were more open to the world around. They kept at less of a distance from other Jews than did the Essenes, membership of whose group was regulated by the surrender of possessions, a novitiate, a period of probation and the taking of an oath (1QS 6.13ff.). Anyone wanting to become an Essene had to undergo strict tests, since in general the other Jews were regarded as children of darkness. By contrast, the Jesus movement regarded them as 'lost sheep of the house of Israel' (Matt. 10.6), and sought them out. This difference becomes obvious when we see how little the Jesus movement stood out from the rest of Judaism and how little it was separated from it. The Essenes had much more of a separatist attitude, but they were still beyond question a part of Judaism. This was even more the case with the Jesus movement.

4. Summary

Our investigation of the local communities has shown that they are to be understood exclusively in terms of their complementary relationship to the wandering charismatics. The radical attitude of the wandering charismatics was possibly only on the basis of the material support offered to them by the local communities. To some degree the local communities relieved them of worries about their day-to-day existence. In turn, the local communities could allow themselves to compromise with the world about them because the wandering charismatics maintained such a clear distinction. The two social forms of the Jesus movement were both associated and distinguished by a gradated pattern of norms.

IV. The Role of the Son of Man

The Jesus movement expressed its expectations of the attitude of the bearer of revelation in various christological titles. Thus various expectations and assignations of roles were originally bound up together. The title Son of God stressed involvement in the divine world and the breaking in of transcendence. It therefore appears in stories in which the heavens are opened (Mark 1.9ff.; 9.2ff.) or in which stress is laid on the origin of the Son from the world beyond (Mark 12.1ff.). By contrast, the term Messiah is much more bound up with this world. It has connotations of the expectation of a king who will free Israel. Here the Jesus movement had to cope with rival expectations of a redeemer which were directed towards a powerful, earthly king. It had to work out the special character of Jesus, his suffering and his humiliation, features which just did not fit into the role traditionally assigned to the Messiah. Thus the title Messiah was above all bound up with the cross (e.g. Mark 15.32). The title Son of man linked sayings concerned with both humiliation and exaltation, involvement in the divine world (which was expressed above all in the title Son of God) and suffering on earth (which, paradoxically, was connected with the title Messiah). For this very reason it is the most important title. And there is a further reason for this. The title Messiah usually occurs on the lips of other people in the gospels, while the title Son of God is used by supernatural beings: God and demons. By contrast, the title Son of man is always used by Jesus himself. The title Messiah sees Jesus from an external perspective which needs to be corrected:

Jesus was not the national messianic king. The title Son of God adopts a transcendental perspective. By contrast, the title Son of man expresses the internal perspective of the Jesus movement and is particularly closely connected with it.

1. Constructive conclusions

In contrast to the roles which we have been analysing, we have access to a wealth of direct statements about the Son of man. They can be divided into two groups: sayings about the earthly Son of man and sayings about the future Son of man. The sayings about the earthly Son of man can in turn be divided into two groups. The first group comprises sayings in an 'active' form: here the Son of man transcends the norms of the world around. He breaks the sabbath (Matt. 12.8), he does not observe the regulations about fasting (Matt. 11.18f.) and he forgives sins on his own authority (Matt. 9.6). The second group comprises sayings in a 'passive' form: the Son of man has to suffer under the reactions of the world around. He is rejected by men (Mark 9.31) and gives up his life as a sacrifice for many (Mark 10.45). The statements in the active and in the passive belong together. The Son of man is an outsider in both a positive and a negative sense: on the one hand he transcends society and its norms; on the other he suffers from being rejected by it. He is given authority, and is rejected. However, this dichotomy is soon transcended: as the eschatological judge he will suddenly and unexpectedly appear in a new role (Mark 14.62; Matt. 24.27ff.) and will gather together his elect (Matt. 13.41; Mark 13.27), despite the fact that no one will know for certain whether or not they are numbered among the elect (Matt. 25.31ff.). By then the outcast will become the judges, the powerless will become the rulers and the outsiders will be given general recognition.

2. Analytical conclusions

Many sayings about the attitude of members of the Jesus movement display an unmistakable parallelism to sayings about the Son of man. This parallelism is in fact stressed in the texts.

For example, we read that anyone who wants to be first must be the servant of all. This requirement is based on the example of the Son of man: 'For the Son of man also came not to be served but to serve, and to give his life as a ransom for many' (Mark 10.45). Consequently we are not doing an injustice to the texts if we make a close connection in the following sections between the role of the Son of man and that of his followers. From a sociological perspective, the ethical requirements of the idea of discipleship – a correspondence between Jesus and his followers – become a structural homologue [8] between the attitudes of the wandering charismatics and the local communities on the one hand and that of the Son of man on the other. As a result, the role of the Son of man as an outsider corresponds both positively and negatively to the role of Christians. To take the positive side first: like the Son of man, his disciples transcended the norms of their environment. In practical terms, the fact that the Son of man is lord of the sabbath means that the wandering disciples can break the sabbath in the same way as David, when he was a homeless fugitive (Mark 2.23ff.). Not only the Son of man (Matt. 11.18ff.), but also his disciples put themselves above the regulations for fasting (Mark 2.18ff.). Heavenly authority upon earth is given not only to the Son of man (Mark 2.1ff.), but also to the community (Matt. 18.8) or to Peter (Matt. 16.19). It is an illuminating fact that most of the parallels relate to the role of the wandering charismatics. This is also true of the 'passive' statements. The Son of man is not alone in being homeless and vulnerable (Matt. 8.20). The wandering charismatics, too, have forsaken everything (Mark 10.28). The Son of man is not alone in being persecuted (Mark 9.31); the same is also true of his followers (Matt. 10.19). Outside the synoptic gospels we find the title Son of man only in a confessional situation: according to Acts 7.56, while he was being stoned Stephen saw heaven opened and the Son of man in his exalted glory. James made a similar confession of the Son of man before his execution (Hegesippus in Eusebius, *HE* II. 23.13), as did the blind man who was made to see after his expulsion from the synagogue (John 9.35; cf. Luke 6.22). It is in accordance with this that in his trial before the Sanhedrin Jesus refers to the future Son of man who will appear in power (Mark

14.62). The *Sitz im Leben* of many of the Son of man sayings is in fact 'confession before men' (Mark 8.38). The conflict between 'man' and the 'Son of man' which appears in them does in fact have a social foundation in the conflict between vagabond outsiders and 'human' society. Understandably enough, the most scanty parallels are those between the future glory of the Son of man and his followers. Here too, however, we can find similarities. The twelve will participate in the future glory of the Son of man:

> In the new world, when the Son of man shall sit on his glorious throne, you who have followed me will also sit on twelve thrones, judging the twelve tribes of Israel (Matt. 19.28).

All these parallels between sayings about the Son of man and early Christian wandering charismatics (and community members) cannot be coincidence. Evidently the images of the Son of man christology had a significant social function. Above all in the figure of the Son of man, early Christian wandering charismatics were able to interpret and come to terms with their own social situation: within small groups of believers they were regarded as authorities and appointed new norms and rules; within society as a whole they were despised and persecuted outsiders. A resolution of the conflict between the role of the outsider and that of the authority was expected in the future. At that time the whole of society would recognize the authority of the wandering charismatic. The ambivalence of the sayings about exaltation and those about humiliation in the Son of man christology is a structural homologue of an inevitable conflict of roles for the early Christian wandering charismatics. From time to time the sayings go beyond being a structural homologue. The wandering charismatics identified themselves with the destiny of the Son of man. They believed that the Son of man himself underwent the same fate as they did:

> Whoever is ashamed of me and of my words in this adulterous and sinful generation, of him will the Son of man also be ashamed, when he comes in the glory of his Father with the holy angels (Mark 8.38).

The explicit emphasis on the 'words of the Son of man' points to those who handed on the words of Jesus, the first Christian preachers. We could therefore paraphrase as follows: whoever rejects the Son of man and those who proclaim his words . . . Thus the rejection of the Son of man, like the rejection of the wandering charismatics, has eschatological consequences in the final judgment:

> And if anyone will not receive you or listen to your words . . . truly I say to you, it shall be more tolerable on the day of judgment for the land of Sodom and Gomorrah than for that town (Matt. 10.14ff.).

There is even a saying in which the earliest Christian preachers set themselves above the Son of man:

> And whoever says a word against the Son of man will be forgiven, but whoever speaks against the Holy Spirit will not be forgiven, either in this age or in the age to come (Matt. 12.32).

The Holy Spirit represents the wandering preachers and the prophetic spirit to which they give expression. The Didache already interprets the saying in this sense (11.7). Thus the meaning is that anyone who has failed to recognize the Son of man at work on earth has a further chance to arrive at the truth through their preaching. This close connection between the Son of man and the wandering charismatics raises the question whether the Son of man was 'merely' the externalized, normative 'super-ego' of the wandering charismatics, whether they shaped their lives in heteronomous fashion as a 'copy' of the role of the Son of man, in effect constructing the picture of the Son of man in accordance with their own role. The great parable of the Son of man gives some grounds for an answer. It shows that the authority of the Son of man does not set out to be an external authority. The patterns of behaviour expected by the Son of man are expected independently of faith in the Son of man or even of an identification with him. For in the final judgment the Son of man will judge all men and say:

> I was hungry and you gave me food. I was thirsty and you gave me drink. I was a stranger and you welcomed me, I was naked and you clothed me, I was sick and you visited me, I was in prison and you came to me (Matt. 25.35f.).

But those who are asked the question will reply in amazement,

'Where did we help you?' And they will be given the answer: 'As you did it to one of the least of these my brethren, you did it to me' (Matt. 25.40). Independent action is therefore expected. A degree of autonomy is part of the expectation of the role of the Son of man among his followers.

3. Comparative conclusions

There is also evidence for the idea of the Son of man in Palestine outside earliest Christianity. It appears for the first time in Daniel 7, where it is connected with a dualism between the succession of world empires (symbolized by animals) and the future kingdom of Israel (symbolized by the Son of man). Here too we may conjecture structural homologues between conceptions and social reality. Thus the rule of the Son of man in Dan. 7.15ff. is interpreted in terms of the rule of the Israelites (the 'saints'). There can be no doubt that those who handed down the traditions of the book of Daniel were themselves intent on rule. Moreover, the transformation of monistic, immanent Old Testament thought into a crude dualism of ages following one another in temporal succession can best be conceived of among groups whose relationship to Israel as a whole was a dualistic form of life: they lived in exclusive conventicles which were clearly marked out from the contemporary environment.[9] Among these groups, the reigning empires were rejected as bestial, and there was a longing for the true realm of 'men'. It was to come soon. But expectations proved deceptive. The true kingdom remained hidden. Accordingly in the Similitudes of Ethiopic Enoch, which were written later, there is emphasis on the hiddenness of the pre-existent Son of man. If those who handed on the apocalyptic hope remained hidden, the transcendent figure to whom they were related had inevitably to remain hidden also. Things were different in the Jesus movement. The Son of man had already appeared. The kingdom of 'men' had already begun. This made speculations about a pre-existent Son of man already unnecessary. It is certainly no coincidence that those structural homologues which can be demonstrated mostly relate to the earthly Son of man. His appearance on earth was the decisive new experience.

4. Summary

All these three types of conclusion thus combine to suggest that
the figure of the Son of man was central for the Jesus movement.
His situation corresponded to their situation. Here belief and
practice formed an indissoluble whole.[10] The unity of this whole
was deliberate. It formed the focal point of the idea of discipleship. It is noteworthy that one of the features of the expectation
of the Son of man among his followers was that he was independent of them. Consequently sociological analysis cannot answer
the question who the Son of man is, whatever other contribution
it may make. It can, however, demonstrate the great significance
of belief in the Son of man for the social life of the earliest
Christian communities.

Part Two

Analysis of Factors: The Effects of Society on the Jesus Movement

A sociological analysis of factors in earliest Christianity is concerned with the reciprocal interaction between Jewish society in Palestine and the Jesus movement. Four factors need to be distinguished here: socio-economic, socio-ecological, socio-political and socio-cultural. Socio-economic factors are the organization of work and the distribution of its products between productive workers and those who enjoy the profits; socio-ecological factors are the results of the interplay between man and nature as expressed in the relationship between city and country and in the trading pattern of a country. Socio-political factors include the structures of government in Palestine, i.e., the opportunities of various groups and institutions for imposing their will as a general law, claiming legitimacy for it and overcoming opposition by force. Socio-cultural factors include all values, norms and traditions which give a group self-awareness and identity. By 'identity' we mean that a positive picture of a group is constructed on the basis of an adequate consensus and is balanced with the picture of other groups which has been arrived at. The terminological stress on the prefix 'socio-' in each case is meant to emphasize that the factors under investigation do not have an immediate effect on human behaviour, but make their impact through the 'totality' of all social interconnections. There is some justification in isolating different aspects, even if such a procedure is artificial. For we cannot achieve a direct understanding of the 'totality' of all social interconnections without confusing partial associations with the whole.

Simply by reason of the methodology employed, the individual sections concerned with analysing factors are constructed in the same way. First of all there is a description of a phenomenon of the Jesus movement. Here it is assumed that while there is a connection with the particular factors described, that does not mean that a phenomenon is exclusively conditioned by these factors or that these factors are significant only in terms of the phenomenon under investigation. We presuppose only that the phenomenon under investigation in each case will be a particularly good illustration of the significance of economic, ecological, political or cultural factors. The second stage will be to collect analogies from contemporary Judaism to the phenomenon under investigation. Underlying this procedure is the methodological presupposition that the more widespread a phenomenon is in society, the more it is influenced by that society. This provides compelling reasons for enquiring into social causes; what these are remains open. It is often the analogies which provide a first indication, since the social conditioning of a phenomenon often emerges more clearly in contemporary parallels than in the Jesus movement itself. The third stage is to investigate 'intentions', i.e., deliberate attitudes adopted in the texts towards supposed social conditioning. The methodological presupposition behind this is that there cannot be any connections between social reality and spiritual phenomena of which those involved in them were not aware, even if their awareness took a different form from our own – at the same time, though, we cannot rule out unconscious connections. Only after these first three stages can we begin to make a direct analysis of the hypothetical causes. This division of the investigation into four stages is meant to demonstrate that the phenomena associated with the Jesus movement cannot be brought into a direct association with their social causes: the procedure must always be indirect, by means of contemporary analogies and the deliberate awareness of those involved. Wherever conclusions are drawn about social causes by means of analogies, the sociological analysis is limited to typical, recurrent and analogous features. An explanation is given of those features which the Jesus movement had in common with contemporary movements, and not its individual and irreplaceable characteristics. In taking into account the intentions of those involved, we may suppose that the connection between social reality and spiritual phenomena is to be seen not only as the effect of a situation on the movement but also as the response of the movement to that situation.

v. Socio-economic Factors

1. The phenomenon

Socio-economic factors were responsible for the most striking phenomenon of the Jesus movement: the social rootlessness of the wandering charismatics. By 'social rootlessness' I mean that the followers of Jesus left their ancestral homes, breaking more or less abruptly with established norms.[11] There is clear evidence for this phenomenon in the gospels themselves. Peter says on behalf of all the disciples, 'See, we have left everything and followed you' (Mark 10.28). Nor should we think only of the group of twelve disciples. In addition to them there were the seven in Jerusalem (Acts 6.5f.) and the five in Antioch (Acts 13.1f.). Luke also records the sending out of seventy wandering charismatics, who had to follow the same rules as the twelve apostles (Luke 10.1ff.; 9.1ff.). The apostles include not only the twelve but Paul and Barnabas (Acts 14.4, 14), Andronicus and Junias (Rom. 16.7), and any missionary who observes 'the teaching of the gospel' on his wanderings (Didache 11.3f.). The limitation of the title to the twelve itself represents a polemical demarcation against an excess of wandering 'apostles' (Luke 21.8; Rev. 2.2). Nor is the title 'apostle' the only indication. Wandering charismatics could also call themselves 'disciples of the Lord'. According to Papias (in Eusebius, *HE* III. 39.4) they and their 'disciples' (!) handed on the traditions about Jesus. The gospels clearly connect the term in Matt. 8.21 and 10.42 with wandering charismatics. Other titles are 'prophets' (Matt. 5.12; 10.41; Didache 11.3ff.), 'righteous' (Matt. 10.41) and 'teachers' (Acts 13.1; Didache 13.2). This variation points to the great breadth of the type of social behaviour underlying them. The texts do not wholly conceal the economic factors behind this social behaviour: those who are called to be disciples include 'the labourers and the heavy-laden' (Matt. 11.28), the beggar Bartimaeus (Mark 10.52), Peter, who is frustrated in his calling (Luke 5.1ff.), and the sons of Zebedee whose father was a 'poor fisherman' according to the Gospel of the Nazarenes.[12] Indeed the fishermen of Lake Tiberias as a class belonged among those 'penniless sailors' who were involved in a rebellion at the beginning of the Jewish war (Josephus, *Vita* 12, §66). The possessed man of Gadara was also prepared to become a disciple. He became a wandering preacher in the region of the Decapolis (Mark 5.18ff.). By contrast, while those who had possessions sympathized with Jesus (like the rich young man and Zacchaeus the tax collector), they shrank from taking the step of becoming complete disciples (Mark 10.22; Luke 19.1ff.), unlike the petty official Levi (Mark 2.13ff.). What we know of the family of Jesus points to 'insignificant people', who lived in difficult circumstances as a peasant class (Hegesippus in Eusebius, *HE* III. 20.2ff.). Social rootlessness could thus be connected with socio-economic pressure. A look at analogous phenomena in contemporary society may serve to confirm this supposition.

2. Analogies

We can find instances of social rootlessness both in the renewal movements within Judaism (the Qumran community, the resistance fighters, prophetic movements) and in the widespread instances of disintegration (emigrants and new settlers, robbers and beggars). Among emigrants and Essenes, evasive attitudes were dominant; both groups left their homes to settle elsewhere. Robbers and resistance fighters adopted predominantly aggressive attitudes, whereas beggars and the prophetic movements looked for support. Both the latter looked for the help of others, beggars for human alms and the followers of the prophets for divine intervention. We can therefore make a theoretical distinction between six phenomena of social rootlessness:

	Evasion	Aggression	Support
Evidence of disintegration	Emigrants New settlers	Robbers	Beggars Vagabonds
Renewal movements	Qumran community	Resistance fighters	Prophetic movements

(i) *Evasive behaviour* The size of the diaspora shows how great emigration must have been. Jews were driven abroad as mercenaries, slaves, fugitives or penniless men in search of a new basis for existence. In AD 41 Claudius had to forbid Jews entry into Alexandria (*CPJ* 153, 96f.). Many must have been prepared to leave their ancestral homeland. This was the only way in which the Herods were able to found their numerous new cities and open up new territories (Caesarea, Sebaste, Sepphoris, Caesarea Philippi, Phasaelis, Bathyra and district, Archelais, Antipatris, Tiberias). For the city of Tiberias which was founded in AD 19/20, Antipas resorted to 'men without means who were brought from all over the country' (*Antt.* 18.2.3, §37). Thus shortly before the period of Jesus' ministry there were in Galilee men without possessions and possibly even without homes. The Qumran community by the Dead Sea will also have recruited some of its members from such men. According to an account by Pliny the Elder, there came to it day by day 'men who were weary of life, and were driven thither by the billows of fortune' (*Natural History* V, 15, §73). According to Josephus, those with and without possessions alike could be found there (*Antt.* 18.1.5, §20). The need for this religiously motivated form of 'emigration' must have been intensive around the beginning of the Christian era. The settlement by the Dead Sea, destroyed by an earthquake in 31 BC, was rebuilt during the rule of Archelaus (4 BC to AD 6).

(ii) *Aggressive behaviour* The gospels take account of robbers (Luke 10.30ff.), as do the Essenes, who sought protection against them with weapons (*BJ* s.8.4, §125). Agrippa I or Agrippa II boasted of defeating them (*OGIS* 424). Many of these so-called 'robbers' were in fact resistance fighters. There is evidence of their activity from the time of Herod's accession to power to the Jewish war. They drew their recruits from the farmers who were no longer able to pay their taxes (*Antt.* 18.8.4, §274), from those in debt (*BJ* 2.17.6, §§424ff.), and from the poor (*BJ* 4.4.3, §241). The fact that they come particularly into prominence· under Cumanus (AD 48–52) and that this development continues up to the Jewish revolt will be connected with the great famine of AD 46–48 and its devastating consequences for many of the lower classes.[13]

(iii) *The search for support*   There is evidence of begging in the New Testament (Mark 10.46ff.; Luke 14.16ff., etc.) and in the Mishnah (Peah 8.7–9). Most of those who were sick or possessed will have lived by begging. The wave of demon possession at that time may have been connected with the crisis in Jewish society in Palestine; the economic factors leading to begging (cf. Luke 16.3) are obvious. To the same causes may also be traced more exalted forms of the search for support: for example, the followers of the numerous prophets who appeared in the first century, promising a repetition of the great miracles of the Old Testament and leading their followers into the wilderness, were 'simple people' (*Antt.* 20.8.6, §§168f.) and 'men without means' (*BJ* 7.9.1, §438). Those who were tied by their possessions to existing conditions had little reason for such eccentric undertakings.

(iv) *Summary*   At the time of Jesus there were many socially rootless people in Palestine. Many lived in unconscious readiness to leave their ancestral homes. They included the disciples of Jesus. But these represented only a variant of possible behaviour. Anyone who was dissatisfied with things as they were could become a criminal or a healer, a beggar or a prophet, a man possessed or an exorcist. He could identify himself with a new form of Judaism or lose his identity completely and become a helpless victim of 'demons'. No sociological explanation can explain why some chose one form of social rootlessness and others another. It can, however, make the morass of social rootlessness comprehensible by referring to the crisis in Jewish Palestinian society. We must remember that social rootlessness is to be found everywhere. Only absolute force could prevent it. However, its increase in the Palestine of the time can hardly be regarded as normal. As it was widespread throughout society, it will also have had social causes.

3. Intentions

An unmistakable pointer to the socio-economic background to social rootlessness is the fact all the renewal movements within Judaism which drew their recruits from those who had no roots in society were critical of society: in various ways they criticized both riches and possessions. A programme can be seen among Essenes and resistance fighters, but the Jesus movement was characterized by a certain 'lack of principle'.[14]

(i) The internal order of the *Qumran community* represented a definite reaction to a society in which the rich had a built-in advantage in the struggle for possessions:

> They despise riches, and their community of goods is truly admirable; you will not find one among them who has more possessions than another. They have a rule that anyone who wants to enter the sect must hand over his property to the community (*BJ* 2.8.3, §122).

All the goods which were important for sustaining life were produced jointly, in isolation from the rest of the world. The community was relatively independent of the outside world; consequently its members could not accept food from outsiders without paying for it, and begging was strictly prohibited. Rather, each individual member was totally dependent on the community. This dependence was in turn the basis of an ascetic discipline. Offences against the norms of the community were punished with material sanctions: for example, the penalty for sleeping during general assemblies was expulsion for a period of ten days; for irregular absence or for spitting, thirty days; for nakedness, six months; for false information about one's possessions, one year. In addition, rations were cut by a quarter, probably for life (1QS 6.24–7.25). Expulsion was a threat to life. As accepting food from strangers was forbidden, a precarious existence had to be eked out on what plants were available. As a result, many starved (*BJ* 2.8.8, §143). Faced with such drastic punishments, people obeyed. Here we see one of the problems facing many attempts at forming a community: the price of consistent observance of the common rules was total dependence on the society and its means of production. The situation of the Essenes scattered throughout the country was rather different. They had to pay two days' wages a month to the community for the support of the weaker ones (CD 14.12ff.).

(ii) *The resistance fighters* did not withdraw from society, but sought a redistribution of possessions within society by means of revolution. Consequently, when they entered Jerusalem they destroyed all the records of debts (*BJ* 2.17.6, §427) and fought against the rich, 'ostensibly in defence of freedom, but in reality simply to gain plunder' (*Antt.* 18.1.1, §7). One victim of their terror campaign among the rich was Zechariah the son of Baruch (*BJ* 4.5.4, §335). His murder is sharply condemned in the synoptic tradition (Matt. 23.35). It is regarded as the last of the wickednesses which began with the murder of Cain; after it there is only the last judgment to come.

(iii) The attitude of the *Jesus movement* to possessions and riches was ambivalent. On the one hand there was criticism of riches (e.g. Mark 10.25; Luke 6.24f., etc.), and on the other the movement profited from them. Support was accepted from the well-to-do wife of an official in Herod's administration (Luke 8.3), from Joseph of Arimathea (Mark 15.43), from a rich woman who was a sinner (Luke 7.36ff.) and from Zacchaeus, the chief tax-collector (Luke 19.1ff.). 'Make friends with the mammon of unrighteousness' (Luke 16.9), went the slogan. This ambivalence can be seen as a sign of the 'lack of principle' in the Jesus movement (H. Braun): renunciation of riches was not an essential condition of salvation, but it could be required in particular instances. This position can also be derived from the social situation of the Jesus movement: wandering charismatics without possessions could make a credible condemnation of riches; but as charismatic beggars they were also concerned that they should have their share of the produce of the land. The two things went well together. The generosity of many rich people could be encouraged by playing on their consciences over their riches. In any case these were the 'hated rich', tax-collectors, prostitutes, outsiders, whose riches had been gained by questionable means. Of course their generosity also benefited the poor. However, the wandering charismatics set clear priorities, for 'you always have the poor with you, and whenever you will, you can do good to them; but you will not always have me' (Mark 14.7; cf. Didache 13.4).

(iv) *Summary* Within the religious renewal movements we find three different answers to the problem of how to sustain life: an over-disciplined productive community, a social programme of revolutionary change and a group of wandering charismatics living on alms. Here disciplined work, robbery and begging were in each case elevated to a higher level and carried on on the basis of religious motivation. The criticism of riches in all three movements indicates that socio-economic tensions were factors in their development.

4. Causes

First, we should call attention to one misunderstanding of 'economic explanations'. One often comes across the rather naive idea that economic pressure leads to changes of attitude and protest predominantly among the lowest classes. In reality, people are activated above all when their situation threatens to deteriorate or when improvements are in sight: only those who know or can expect better living standards react sensitively to poverty and wretchedness. Thus all trends towards improvements or declines in living standards instigate action, and they can emerge in all levels of society. This is why in many protest movements we find members of the upper classes – often in leading roles; for the most part members of an upper class whose position has been undermined. For example, the Qumran community was formed from priestly aristocrats who had been forced out of power. The leaders of the resistance movements from Hezekiah to John of Gischala often had an astonishingly good relationship with the upper classes in Jerusalem (to which they were perhaps related): true, initially John the rebel leader was poor (*BJ* 2.21.1, §585),

but he did come from a formerly well-to-do family.[15] Menahem,
the leader of the community in Antioch mentioned in Acts 13.1,
as an intimate of Prince Antipas, was a member of the upper class
and could have been involved in the troubles connected with his
downfall and exile. Thus while the poor may be the basis of social
unrest (and even that is not always true), the impoverished rich or
the groups whose status has been made insecure are often its
motive force. Consequently we must pay less attention to the
absolute extent of economic pressure than to its increase in the
case of particular classes; less attention to established levels than
to upward and downward trends; less attention to static structures than to change. The causes of these socio-economic changes
were: natural catastrophes, over-population, the concentration of
possessions and competing tax systems.[16] For a large part of the
population these changes meant an increase in socio-economic
pressure.

(i) Most of the *famines* attested by Josephus fall in the first century BC: a drought (65), a hurricane (64), an earthquake (31),
epidemics (29), a famine (25). However, Mark 13.8 mentions
earthquakes and famines as signs of the present. And there is
evidence for a great famine under Claudius about AD 46/47 (*Antt.*
20.2.5, §§51ff.; Acts 11.28); during his reign there were failures in
food supplies generally within the empire. The natural catastrophes of the first century AD may have had more serious consequences than those of the previous century. Herod lessened the
consequences of catastrophes by selling his private possessions
and remitting taxes (*Antt.* 15.9.1f., §§299ff., 365). We hear nothing of comparable state aid from the period of direct Roman
administration (after AD 6), but only of private initiatives (Acts
11.28; *Antt.* 20.2.5, §§51ff.). This had momentous consequences,
as is shown by the increase in robbery and rebellion in sub-
sequent years.

(ii) In addition, we must reckon with the possibility of a degree
of *over-population* in Palestine. Aristeas (§133) stressed the density of settlement in Palestine and Josephus the density of population in Galilee (*BJ* 3.3.2, §43; *Vita* 45, §230). Certainly Galilee

was more densely populated than neighbouring regions in the
north and east ruled over by Philip. Philip's income was only 100
talents, whereas that of Antipas was 200 (*Antt.* 17.11.4, §318ff.).
But that does not mean much. The result of investigations into
agriculture is more significant; according to these, more than 97%
of land in Palestine was under cultivation at that time.[17]
Moreover, there seems to have been a lack of new areas for
settlement in the time of Herod: he settled Jews in territories
outside Jewish tribal territory (*Antt.* 17.2.2f., §§23ff.; *BJ* 3.3.1,
§36), and used irrigation for the cultivation of new land in the
Jordan valley (*Antt.* 16.5.3, §145).

(iii) A progressive *concentration of possessions* probably heightened the struggle over the distribution of wealth in the first
century AD. Herod had taken over a very great deal of land
through confiscation (*Antt.* 17.11.2, §307). These possessions
were later sold by the Romans (*Antt.* 17.13.5, §355; 18.1.1, §2).
Only those in possession of some capital were in a position to
buy. The rich became even richer. Their resources could produce
goods for export. For a long time the export of balsam had been
in the hands of the ruling classes (Diodorus Siculus II. 48.9; *BJ*
1.18.5, §361; *Antt.* 15.4.2, §96). Herodian princes provided the
neighbouring Hellenistic cities with grain (Acts 12.20ff.; *Vita* 24,
§119). Oil was exported to Syria at a profit (*BJ* 2.21.2, §591). In
any case, the great figures in the land owned the most fertile
areas. Salome, Herod's sister, had an income of sixty talents a
year merely from estates in Jamnia and Phasaelis, which were
later taken over by the Roman empire (*Antt.* 17.11.5, §321). By
contrast, Peraea and Galilee brought in only 200 talents (*Antt.*
17.11.4, §318ff.). Export, on which the income of the real tycoons
was based, flourished. This is the only explanation for the very
rapid growth of the port of Caesarea from the time of its founding
in 10 BC. The peace of Augustus was favourable to trade. It is
therefore no coincidence that in the parable of the talents, the
rich man who lends the money – he has features resembling
Archelaus – has good connections abroad. Big business could be
done only through exporting. The pessimistic statement at the
end of the parable needs no comment: 'To every one who has,

more will be given; but from him who has not, even what he has will be taken away' (Luke 19.26).

(iv) Socio-economic pressure is above all the result of a *struggle for the distribution of goods* between the producers and those who make the profits. This is not a confrontation between two self-contained classes. Rather, the struggle continues within the groups which enjoy the profits. *Élites* made up of both Romans and native Palestinians competed for their share in the exploitation of the land. This rivalry was perhaps the decisive reason for the explosive situation in Palestine. The significance of the state tax is illuminated by the events connected with Caligula's crazy attempt to erect his effigy in the temple in Jerusalem (AD 39/40). Because of the protracted demonstrations in the protest at the action there were fears that 'neglect of agriculture would inevitably result in more banditry because they (i.e. the peasants who took part in the demonstrations) would not be able to pay the taxes' (*Antt.* 18.8.4, §274). Thus those who were driven to leave their homeland were often exiled because they were in debt over tax. They felt that they were delivered over to the creditors without any form of protection (Matt. 5.25f.). The remission of debts could become an image of divine grace (Matt. 18.23ff.). And the praise of the unjust steward, who takes it upon himself to reduce the amounts owed by his master's debtors, only makes sense if the remission of debt is seen from the start as something positive (Luke 16.1ff.). Those who were in debt could take refuge with the freedom fighters. Their programme included release from debt, as the destruction of the debtors' records in the Jerusalem archives shows (*BJ* 2.17.6, §427). They rejected the payment of tax in principle, unless it was made to Yahweh. They regarded it as 'shameful to continue to pay tax to the Romans and to recognize mortal men as their masters, as well as God' (*BJ* 2.8.1, §118). This was certainly a radical consequence to draw from the first commandment: only a minority thought in this way. However, numerous complaints show that the taxes were generally felt to be oppressive: after Herod's death his successor was required to do away with certain taxes (*Antt.* 17.8.4, §205). Complaints were made to Augustus about the excessive poll-tax

(*Antt.* 17.11.2, §308). The Palestinians and the Syrians united in asking Tiberius to reduce the taxes (Tacitus, *Annals* II.42.). The Jews had every reason for this. For Augustus had in fact remitted a quarter of the taxes in Samaria but not in the province of Judaea, since there had been rebellions here after the death of Herod (*Antt.* 17.11.4, §319). The level of taxes was meant to be felt as a punishment. No wonder that the resistance movement developed at that time as a protest against the payments of tax (*Antt.* 18.1.1, §4). Again, refusal to pay taxes was the decisive cause of the Jewish rebellion *BJ* 5.9.4, §405; 2.17.1, §405). Tax remissions under Herod (*Antt.* 15.10.4, §365; 16.2.5, §64), Vitellius (*Antt.* 18.4.3, §90) and Agrippa I (*Antt.* 19.6.3, §299) show how oppressive the taxes were. They served the purpose of lessening social and political pressures. Here, too, the situation of the population had probably become worse in the first century AD, if conditions in the new Jewish settlement of Batanaea are anything to go by. During the life of Herod, the new settlers enjoyed freedom from tax. This was one of the indispensable initial concessions for new pioneers. However, under his successor Philip, insignificant taxes were raised (*Antt.* 17.2.1f., §§23ff.). Agrippa I and II 'oppressed them with taxes', but the Romans went even further (*Antt.* 17.2.2, §28). There were religious taxes in addition to the state ones. The most important source of income for the priests, the tithe, was not a purely theoretical demand. It was part of the programme for the Pharisees (Luke 18.12; Matt. 23.23). There were vigorous struggles over its distribution:

> The high priests finally reached such a pitch in their arrogance and their audacity that they did not hesitate to send their servants to the threshing floors and have them take away the tithes due to the priests; the result of this was that the poorer of the priests perished of starvation (*Antt.* 20.8.8, §181; cf. 20.9.2, §§206f.).

During the disturbances before the Jewish war the income probably grew even smaller. So the dispute over it became even more furious. The interest of the Jerusalem aristocracy in the tithe is also evident from the fact that at the very beginning of the Jewish war a commission was sent to Galilee, which was, among other things, to collect the tithe (*Vita* 12, §63). More decisive

than the quantitative addition of the two tax demands was the
fact that they were in competition with one another: the Romans
had military power to back up their demands, while the priestly
aristocracy justified their taxation on ideological grounds. Two
things followed from this. First, the more the effective political
power of the native aristocracy declined, the more they had to
compensate for their lack of real power by emphasis on the
legitimacy of their claims. They could emphasize this legitimacy
by stress on the law, since the law guaranteed and legitimated the
very existence of the priestly aristocracy by the will of God.
Objectively speaking, a degree of legal rigorism was in their interest. Here the two parties of the aristocratic Sadducees and the
legalistic Pharisees, formerly at enmity with one another, could
make common cause, so that in the first century AD their quarrels
could retreat into the background: for economic reasons the
priestly aristocracy inevitably approved of what the Pharisees
propagated on religious grounds (e.g. the payment of the tithe).
The liberal Jesus movement, on the other hand, ran contrary to
the objective interests of the aristocracy, as it undermined the law
from within by claiming priestly privileges for its charismatics
(Mark 2.23ff.; Didache 13.3ff.), raising fundamental questions
about the necessity to pay religious taxes and in fact only paying
church taxes by way of a compromise (Matt. 17.24ff.; 23.23). A
further consequence of the competition of the two tax systems
was that ethnocentricity and xenophobia proved to be welcome
channels into which the aristocracy could divert the aggressions
nurtured by the struggle over the distribution of property, direct-
ing them against the Romans. Here the aristocracy was playing
with fire, and Agrippa II was probably right in giving it a share of
responsibility for the disturbances, even though its supporter
Josephus dismisses these charges (*BJ* 2.16.2, §§336ff.). However
much the aristocracy might have been interested in an agreement with the Romans, for reasons of domestic politics they could
hardly have done without them as the object of national hostility.
Here the Jesus movement was swimming against the stream. It
included the hated tax collectors among its numbers and spoke of
loving enemies and being reconciled with them. It expressed its
eirenic attitude in the dispute over the payment of taxes: 'Render

to Caesar the things that are Caesar's, and to God the things that are God's' (Mark 12.17). This is usually understood to refer on the one hand to specific payments to the state and on the other to spiritual, religious obligations. It could also mean, however, that taxes are to be paid to Caesar and the tithe (and other offerings) to God. In any event, the followers of Jesus would reject the slogan of the resistance movement, that payment of tax to the Romans was incompatible with God's sole rule.

To stress the point yet again: the rivalry of two systems of taxation constantly brought into question the legitimacy of state taxes. The double taxation was itself a burden, and its lack of legitimation inevitably caused resentment. This problem of legitimation brought about a direct connection between economic problems and religious problems, i.e. the question of God's rule and Israel's election. The economic situation was interpreted in the light of this tradition.

5. Summary

The *pax Romana* of the age of Augustus had positive consequences for Palestine in terms of trade and commerce, which led to changes in the socio-economic structure of the country. On the one hand, new groups found their way into the upper class, e.g. those connected with the family of Herod (Mark 3.6; 12.13), while on the other the situation for many ordinary people became much worse. The trends upwards and downwards shattered traditional values and norms and called forth a longing for renewal. The Jesus movement was one of the renewal movements. We find in it both members of the new upper class and their sympathizers – the wife of the Herodian official Chuza (Luke 8.3), an intimate of Antipas (Acts 13.1), Zacchaeus the chief tax collector (Luke 19.1ff.) – and members of the middle classes who were threatened with debt and a decline in fortunes: farmers, fishermen and craftsmen. Here there were often very definite reasons for leaving hearth and home. Without question there were economic reasons for the various patterns of social rootlessness within the renewal movements inside Judaism. But once they had been established, they could be associated with new motivations and interpretations. Nevertheless, the thoroughgoing criticism of riches and possessions in all three renewal movements shows that economic reasons never retreated completely into the background. Such reasons must also be taken into account in the case of the Jesus movement. In assessing it, it is important to note that the poverty to be found among the lower classes is not sufficient in itself to explain the social and religious movements in Palestine during the first century. The threat of poverty was often more of an incentive to rebellion than its actual presence. Throughout history the intolerable has always been tolerated for an astonishingly long time. Thus the social context of the renewal movements within the Judaism of the first century AD was not so much the lowest class of all as a marginal middle class, which reacted with peculiar sensitivity to the upward and downward trends within society which were beginning to make themselves felt.

VI. Socio-ecological Factors

Tension between the cities and the country became an important factor of social development at the latest after the upsurge in cities in the Hellenistic period. This is also true of Palestine, even if the socio-ecological structure of the land cannot be expressed in terms of the opposition between city and country. A distinction must be made on the one hand between the Hellenistic city states and the main Jewish cities (and indeed lesser Jewish communities), and on the other between settled areas and trackless hills and wildernesses.[18]

1. The phenomenon

The Jesus movement originally had close ties with the country. It was a Galilean movement (cf. Mark 14.70; Acts 1.11; 2.7). The synoptic tradition is located in small and often anonymous Galilean places. We hear nothing of the more important towns, like Sepphoris, Tiberias, Cana, Jotapata or Gischala. Chorazim is mentioned only to be consigned to hell (Matt. 11.20). It is even more illuminating that where Hellenistic cities are in fact mentioned, Jesus enters only the surrounding territory, and not the cities themselves. He touches on the 'villages of Caesarea Philippi' (Mark 8.27), the 'region of Tyre' (Mark 7.24, 31), the 'country of the Gerasenes' (Mark 5.1). He goes through the Decapolis without entering the actual ten cities (Mark 7.31). This restriction to the district surrounding the cities may be historical, since it is contrary to the situation obtaining in the period after

Easter: at an early stage there was a church in Tyre (Acts 21.3f.).
The Jesus movement was originally confined to the country areas.
We hear a good deal about farmers, fishermen, vintners and shepherds, and very little about craftsmen and merchants. Mention
of learned men is also rare. They have to be summoned from
Jerusalem to make an appearance in Galilee (Mark 3.22; 7.1).
There was an ambivalent relationship to Jerusalem. On the one
hand, the metropolis soon became the centre of the movement,
while on the other Jerusalem had an evil reputation: it kept killing
the prophets who were sent to it (Luke 13.33ff.). Its temple
would have to give place to a new temple (Mark 14.58). It had
become a den of robbers (Mark 11.15ff.). In my view, the explanation of this phenomenon – the combination of the basis of the
Jesus movement in the country with its ambivalence towards
Jerusalem – is best explained in terms of the conflict between city
and country, especially as there are analogies to it elsewhere.

2. Analogies

Connections can be made between particular renewal movements
and the various ecological structures. The Essenes had their
centre in the wilderness, the zealots were based on hiding places
in the hill-country, while the Jesus movement was to be found in
densely populated areas. The wilderness was of great significance
to prophetic movements. Common to all these groups was their
detachment from Jerusalem.

(i) *John the Baptist* appeared in the wilderness and revived old
dreams of salvation from the wilderness (Isa. 40.3; Mark 1.3). His
ascetic style of life was a deliberate contrast to the luxurious life
of the upper classes in the cities (Matt. 11.7ff.). The Jesus
movement was originally a branch of the baptist movement. It
differed from the latter in its involvement with society and its
refusal to observe a number of ascetic rules (Matt. 11.19; Mark
2.18). In contrast, other prophets led their followers into the
wilderness (*Antt.* 20.8.6, §167; Matt. 24.25f.). An Egyptian led
his adherents through the wilderness to the Mount of Olives. He
promised that the walls of Jerusalen would collapse at his com-

mand (*Antt.* 20.8.6, §170; cf. *BJ* 2.13.5, §§261ff.; Acts 21.38). It is interesting that Jerusalem was regarded as a hostile city, as a new Jericho which had to be conquered before anything else could be done.

(ii) *The Essenes* retreated into the wilderness, there to make ready the way of the Lord (Isa. 40.3 is quoted in 1QS 8.13f.). This was thought to require stricter fulfilment of the law. Others lived dispersed throughout Judaea. Josephus asserts that they were to be found in every 'city' (*BJ* 2.8.4, §124), but he often uses the term 'cities' for the villages of his homeland. Philo is probably more accurate when he writes in his treatise *That Every Good Man is Free* (12, §76) that they are above all to be found in 'villages'.

(iii) *The resistance movements* were obviously based on the country areas. The unrest after the death of Herod was primarily to be found there (*Antt.* 17.10.4, §§269ff.). It only spread to Jerusalem when the country people had streamed there for Pentecost. When the revolt had been put down, those in Jerusalem comforted themselves with the thought that it was 'simply the boldness of the outsiders which had led to it (i.e. the rebellion]; far from intending to besiege the Romans, they themselves were victims of the siege along with the Romans' (*Antt.* 17.10.9, §293). From then on the Romans reinforced their military presence on feast days. Nevertheless, there were continual upheavals as a result of the influx of people from the country (cf. *BJ* 2.12.1, §225; *Antt.* 20.8.5, §165; 20.10.3, §§208ff.). In general the country people were more rebellious than the city-dwellers: leaders of the revolt came from Galilee, like Judas the Galilean (*BJ* 2.8.1, §118); they operated in Idumaea and Arabia, like Tholomaeus (*Antt.* 20.1.1, §5), or in Samaria and Judaea like Eleazar, son of Deinaeus (*Antt.* 20.6.1, §121). They quite deliberately made the Jerusalem aristocracy the victims of their terror, whether through murder (*Antt.* 20.8.5, §§164f.) or through the taking of hostages to free imprisoned resistance fighters (*Antt.* 20.10.3, §§208ff.). During the Jewish revolt, hordes of them entered Jerusalem. Four country groups tyrannized members of the city population whom they suspected of being friendly to the Romans: Galileans under John of Gischala (*BJ* 4.3.1, §§121ff.; 4.9.10, §§558f.), Judaeans under Simon, son of Gioras (*BJ* 2.22.2, §652; 4.9.3, §503), zealots under Eleazar (*BJ* 4.4.1, §§225ff.) – in my view these were chiefly country priests – and a group of Idumaeans (*BJ* 4.4.1, §224). We can only understand the terror they caused if we see it as a means of expressing their long stored up hatred of the city population. From a political and military point of view it was irrational.

3. Intentions

The programmes of all the renewal movements suggest a detachment from the Hellenistic cities and an ambivalent attitude towards Jerusalem. They affirmed the holiness of Jerusalem, but they no longer recognized it as a given fact; rather, it had been surrendered, and the more they contrasted the idea of the holy city with its reality, the more radical their criticism became.

(i) According to Philo, the *Essenes* had a markedly pessimistic view of the (Hellenistic) cities. They feared the dangers of civilization like an infectious germ (*Every Good Man* 12, §76). Philo's remarks are probably somewhat coloured with a longing for the simple life – the *Idylls* of Theocritus were widely read in Alexandria – but he is right in noting the reluctance of the Essenes to make contact with the wider world (cf. 1QS 5.14f.). Jerusalem, too, was part of the unclean world. Granted, the Essenes sent offerings to the temple. But they did not take part in the sacrificial cult; rather, it was rejected as being unclean (*Antt.* 18.1.5, §19; CD 4.18; 5.6; 1QpHab 12.7f. etc.). The city had been defiled by illegitimate priests. The Essenes hoped for radical change, fortifying themselves with the quite remarkable vision of a holy city in which all sexual activity was forbidden (CD 12.1).

(ii) *The resistance fighters*, too, are said to have been completely against contact with the Hellenistic cities. According to the account of the church father Hippolytus, zealots and *sicarii* – both are names for resistance groups – did not go into any city 'so that no one had to go through a gateway with a statue on it' (*Adv. haer.* 9.26). The reason behind this negative attitude was their radical interpretation of the commandment against making images. Its motivation was ethnocentric. They were particularly concerned to stress the Jewish norms. This made Jerusalem all the more important to them. Here they wanted to put things to rights, if necessary by force. So in Jerusalem the zealots proudly called themselves 'benefactors and saviours of the city' (*BJ* 4.3.5, §146). Thoroughgoing reforms were carried out in the temple. A Zadokite again became high priest for the first time since the accession of Herod. It is significant that he came from the country (*BJ* 4.3.8, §§155f.). It is impossible to miss the affront thus made to the high priestly families in the city.

(iii) At first the *Jesus movement* also maintained a marked degree of detachment from the Hellenistic cities. There must have been a move within it to limit all activities to the hinterland of Judaea. One saying warns against going to the Gentiles or entering the towns of the Samaritans (Matt. 10.5f.), while another prophesies that they will not even finish visiting the 'towns' of Israel before the coming of the Son of man (Matt. 10.23). Nevertheless, their attitude towards the neighbouring city states was unlike that of the other renewal movements. These cities could be presented as a model. Thus Tyre and Sidon were expected to be more ready to repent than Chorazin and Bethsaida (Matt. 11.20ff.). There were reminiscences of positive examples from the Old Testament, the widow of Sarepta and Naaman the Syrian (Luke 4.24ff.). True, there was also a good deal of mistrust: the story of the Syro-Phoenician woman shows how much prejudice had to be overcome before men who had for ages taunted each other with bestial epithets came to a mutual understanding (Mark 7.24ff.). However, there were missions in Samaria and Syria at a very early stage (Acts 8.1ff.; 11.20). This mission (even among the Gentiles) was accepted in principle by all, even if not everyone was involved in it (Gal. 2.1ff.). The open attitude towards the Hellenistic cities modified the attitude of the Jesus movement towards Jerusalem: Jerusalem was regarded as the destination of the eschatological pilgrimage of all nations. The temple was to become the house of prayer for all the Gentiles (Mark 11.17). The holy city remained the centre even for the Hellenistic communities (Gal. 2.17ff.; I Cor. 16.3; Rom. 15.25). However, this Jerusalem was no longer thought of anxiously in terms of its holiness over against all the Gentiles. It was the centre of a universalistic Judaism.

4. Causes

The key renewal movements – for the moment leaving Pharisaism on one side – were rooted in the country and dominated by trends hostile to Jerusalem. As the phenomenon was widespread in society, we must consider its social causes: the social conditions producing on the one hand the conservative attitude of Jerusalem in religion and politics, and on the other the more rebellious attitude of the country areas.

(i) The reason for the *conservatism of the inhabitants of Jerusalem* may have been the way in which the whole population in some way or another had a financial interest in the temple. This tie brought about a partial community of interest between the upper classes and the lower classes: both profited from the *status quo*. As a result, outside festival times, when the city was filled with the country population, Jerusalem was a relatively peaceful city. The Roman occupying forces were strengthened by a cohort only on feast days (*BJ* 2.12.1, §224).

(*a*) Almost all the inhabitants of Jerusalem were indirectly dependent on the temple. Cattle-dealers, money-changers, tanners and shoemakers lived off it. The pilgrims brought money into the city and the population provided services for them. The economy of Jerusalem was based on a foreign trade which arose out of religion. Otherwise there were no significant sources of income. The surroundings were not very fertile. There was no industry. The great trade routes ran along the coast or through Transjordania. In any case, religious prejudice was a hindrance to trade. There were import restrictions on pagan luxuries (b.Shab. 14b; j.Pes. 27d, 54ff.; j.Ket. 32c, 4ff.). Ritual prohibitions hampered cattle-dealing (*Antt.* 12.3.4, §§145f.). There were even disputes over the sale of agricultural produce to Gentiles (CD

12.8ff.). Occupations such those of ass-driver, camel-driver, etc., with their trade connections, were discriminated against (Kidd. 4.14; cf. Aristeas §114). Jerusalem lacked an influential merchant class, which by their greater openness could have formed a counterbalance to ethnocentricism and xenophobia. Josephus, the aristocrat from Jerusalem, puts it very clearly: we know nothing of 'trade and commerce' (*C.Ap.* 1.12, 060). At an early stage, at any rate, there was constant commerce between Jerusalem and the outside world by virtue of its position as a capital. Once the Romans had taken over supreme government, however, Caesarea became the seat of state government and its administration. Only the self-government still allowed to the Jews was based on Jerusalem. This meant that the religious significance of the city had to be stressed even more strongly. Without it Jerusalem simply would not have been able to exist. Jerusalem was a city without an adequate basis for its status.

(*b*) Quite a significant proportion of the population was directly dependent on the temple. The temple paid good wages. On one occasion the temple workers went on strike and achieved a 100% rise in wages (b.Yoma 38a). Moreover, wages were paid by the hour (*Antt.* 20.9.7, §220). The reason for the social significance of the temple as the largest employer in Jerusalem was the rebuilding of the temple, which lasted from 20/19 BC to AD 62/64. To begin with, Herod had employed eleven thousand workers (*Antt.* 15.11.2, §390), and according to Josephus (*Antt.* 20.9.7, §§219f.), when the building works were completed new employment had to be found for eighteen thousand. This increase in the numbers involved is all the more remarkable since the extensive work was in fact finished during the reign of Herod. Did the temple employ more people than was absolutely necessary? Even in the time of Herod, the temple building had the character of a job-creating programme: in this way, for example, it could employ a thousand poor priests and put the temple treasure to good economic use.

(*c*) In addition to this, the temple accorded legal privileges to the entire city: the holiness of the city was a viable reason for remission of taxes. A fictitious decree of king Demetrius of Syria, with wide-ranging tax rebates, indicates the trend of the desires

of the inhabitants of Jerusalem (I Macc. 19.25ff.). On two occasions we have specific evidence of tax remissions for Jerusalem:
on the first, Vitellius, legate of Syria, remitted the turnover tax on
fruit sold in the market in Jerusalem (*Antt.* 18.4.3, §90); on the
second, Agrippa I forwent a wealth tax which proved a burden
to the leading houses of Jerusalem (*Antt.* 19.6.3, §299). These
remissions of tax represented a preference for the city over the
country – an essential ingredient of political success.

To sum up: the moderate attitude of the inhabitants of
Jerusalem was based on the common interest of the populace and
the aristocracy in the *status quo* of the city and the temple. By
contrast, all the renewal movements with roots in the country
were inevitably in opposition to the temple, which represented
the existing social and religious system. Jesus prophesied that it
would soon be destroyed and then rebuilt. The Essenes rejected
the sacrificial worship of the temple. The zealots murdered large
numbers of the temple aristocracy and carried through a radical
reform of the temple. The inhabitants of Jerusalem could not
have been interested in such changes. Any disturbances in which
they were involved were connected with the defence of the *status
quo* against attacks from the Romans. There was a concern to
protect the city of the temple from profanation by pagan em-
blems, or there was resistance against using the temple funds for
profane purposes (*Antt.* 18.3.1, §§55ff.; Philo, *Leg. ad Gaium*
36ff., §§290ff.; *Antt.* 18.3.2, §§60ff.; *BJ* 2.14.6, §§293ff.). As the
renewal movements did not accept the temple, and thus ran
counter to the interests of the inhabitants of Jerusalem, they
found it hard to gain a footing in Jerusalem. The same was true of
the Jesus movement. The prophecy of a new temple not built
with hands was certainly not in accord with the interests of those
who were dependent on the temple building, whether directly or
indirectly.

(ii) It is harder to explain *the rebellious attitude of the country
areas* than the moderation of the inhabitants of Jerusalem –
simply because we know less about conditions in the country.
Nevertheless, we can still detect some reasons.

(*a*) Country areas were harder to control. The Roman forces were concentrated in the cities (Caesarea, Samaria, Jerusalem). They seldom got as far as the caves in the hills which from time immemorial had been the refuge of robbers and rebels (from the time of David to that of the Maccabees). It was here that the resistance fighters found a good strategic base (*Antt.* 14.15.5, §§421ff.; 15.10.1, §§346ff.; *BJ* 4.9.4, §§512f.). The Jesus movement, too, found initial success in country areas: it was in Jerusalem that Jesus was arrested and executed.

(*b*) For the most part, the inhabited areas of the Judaean countryside were border territory. By contrast, Jerusalem lay in the heart of Judaea. In any case, it was not far from the adjacent Hellenistic city states: Ashkelon, Ptolemais, Tyre and Sidon lay in the west and the Decapolis in the east. All these cities had Jewish minorities, whose members often lived in the surrounding countryside rather than in the cities themselves (this is probably the reason why Jesus always went to these areas and not to the actual cities). This situation may be inferred from two events. On the outbreak of the Jewish war, the Jews were outside the city walls of Scythopolis. Here they were slaughtered in a wood (*BJ* 2.13.3, §§466ff.). We also hear of a conflict with the Philadelphians. The bone of contention was a group of villages in the territory belonging to the city (*Antt.* 20.1.1, §§2ff.). Thus the country people often lived in direct contact with alien cultures. Such frontier areas were fertile ground for both nationalistic and liberal tendencies. Nationalistic tendencies could be found among the resistance movements operating in the country. These movements directed their actions not only against the Romans but also against the adjacent alien population – as happened with Tholomaeus (*Antt.* 20.1.1, §5). By contrast, the Jesus movement displayed liberal tendencies. It gradually opened its ranks to foreigners. We may recall the miracle stories of the Gentile centurion (Matt. 8.5ff.) and the Syro-Phoenician woman (Mark 7.24ff.). Jesus' initially abrupt rejection of the Syro-Phoenician woman with a reference to the priority of the Israelites reflects the tensions between the ethnic groups in the Galilean frontier territory.

(*c*) Economic pressure was probably greater in the country than in the city. In the Letter of James there is a lament over the blatant injustice done to agricultural workers (James 4.4). The parable of the workers in the vineyard is evidence of the rebellious mood among the tenants of the great estates. The Zeno papyri show that produce could be withheld from absent landowners (*CPJ* 6; *PSI* 554). The aggressiveness of the country population towards the masters who profited from their work was often reinforced by absenteeism. For example a certain Crispus had an estate in Transjordania but lived in Tiberias (*Vita* 9, §33). Josephus lived in Rome, but had an estate on the great plains (*Vita* 76, §422). The parables presuppose the absence of the landlord (Luke 16.1ff.; 13.6ff.; 19.1ff.; Mark 12.1ff.). This absenteeism in fact helped on the transition from slavery to colonization,[19] but it had disadvantages for the smaller tenants in Palestine: the absentee landlords – who were often foreigners – were interested only in profit, and not in the prosperity of their possessions.

(iii) *Tensions between city and country* contributed to the failure of the Jesus movement on its first appearance in Jerusalem. This is evident from the account of the passion. The Sanhedrin differed over whether Jesus should be arrested during the feast of the passover: they did not want any unrest among the people (Mark 14.2). These 'people' can only be the countryfolk coming in for the festival. The inhabitants of Jerusalem were always there. According to the narrative of the entry into Jerusalem, Jesus had sympathizers among the pilgrims who had come for the feast. On the other hand, the authorities were already suspicious of his movement because it came from Galilee (Mark 14.67, 70). They regarded it simply as a special instance of the unrest which always crept into the city from the countryside. Two charges were laid against Jesus: that he claimed to be Messiah and that he prophesied about the temple. The aristocracy was very interested whether he was the Messiah (Mark 14.61f.; 15.31f.). Like Pilate (Mark 15.2), they stressed the political aspects of his ministry. The prophecy against the temple, on the other hand, was brought up by anonymous accusers, presumably popular spokesmen (Mark 14.58; 15.29f.). The building workers, among others, must have been disturbed by the forecast of the destruction of the temple – by divine intervention? by sabotage? who could know? Others were tied to the temple by different interests. It is therefore probable that Jesus found himself in conflict not only with the native aristocracy and the Romans but also with the people of Jerusalem. His conflict cannot be expressed in terms of a conflict between the lower classes and the upper classes. It was overlaid with socio-ecological factors. The people of Jerusalem rejected him (Mark 15.11), but he had a sympathizer in Joseph of Arimathea, a member of the country upper class (Mark 15.42). The Jesus movement later found a footing in Jerusalem. Here it was represented by marginal groups: on the one hand by people who had moved from Galilee to settle in Jerusalem (like Peter and James, Gal. 2.18f.), and on the other by the Hellenists, i.e. by Greek-speaking diaspora Jews (Acts 6.1f.; Mark 15.21). There were tensions between the two groups, probably because of socio-economic inequalities: the fishermen and farmers who had moved from Galilee to settle in Jerusalem were probably worse off than those who had moved to Jerusalem from pious motives, so as not to have to live far from the sacred precincts. It is certainly no coincidence that a diaspora Jew made a notable gift to the Jerusalem community (Acts 4.36f.). Givers often wanted to have a say in the use to which their gifts were put. This also seems to have been the case in the Jerusalem community. The Hellenists,[20] whom we must assume to be the major givers, complained that their widows were not being given a fair share in the distribution of provisions. According to Luke, this dispute led to a split in the organization between the groups (Acts 6.1ff.). The dispute was 'resolved' from outside: the Hellenistic group was driven out of Jerusalem (Acts 8.1). However, the communities which it founded abroad continued to support the 'poor' in Jerusalem (Acts 11.27ff.; Gal. 2.10). The socio-economic inequalities between the two groups remained.

5. Summary

Like the other renewal movements within Judaism, the Jesus movement had its roots in the hinterland of Judaea. We can see that it had an ambivalent relationship both to the Judaean capital and to the Hellenistic city states. On the one hand the central position of Jerusalem was maintained, while on the other hand the temple, the centre of Jerusalem, was rejected in its present form. On the one hand the followers of Jesus were mistrustful of the Hellenistic population, while on the other they were surprised by its openness. At an early stage cities became centres of the new movement. A significant local community developed first in Jerusalem, and then in Damascus, Caesarea, Antioch, Tyre, Sidon and Ptolemais (Acts 9.10ff.; 10.1ff.; 11.20ff.; 21.3ff.; 27.3). The Jesus movement found doors opened to them in the Hellenistic cities because they could offer prospects of a resolution of the tensions between Jews and Gentiles: theirs was a universalistic Judaism, which was open to outsiders.

VII. Socio-political Factors

1. The phenomenon

Josephus described the nature of the Jewish community as a 'theocracy', i.e. literally as the rule of God (*c. Ap.* 2.16, §165). In it, God himself theoretically occupied the chief place. This was in accordance with ancient Israelite traditions (cf. I Sam. 8.7; Ps.47; Isa. 33.22; Zeph. 3.15). *De facto*, however, the 'rule of God' was the rule of the priestly aristocracy. So when Josephus elsewhere describes the nature of the Jewish community as an 'aristocracy' (*Antt.* 20.10.1, §229), he is not contradicting himself: the priests claimed to represent God's rule. Not everyone recognized that. The tension between the nominal theocracy and the *de facto* aristocracy became the breeding ground for radical theocratic movements in which the theocracy of Yahweh was played off against its theocratic mediators and their confederates, the priests and the Romans. The Jesus movement was also such a radical theocratic movement. It proclaimed the imminence of the rule of God. And however one twisted it, this rule of God meant the end of all other rule, even the rule of the Romans and the priests. There is good evidence for the conflict with them; the two groups worked together for the execution of Jesus. At a later stage relations with the Romans seem to have been less tense. None of the persecutions of which we know can be laid at their door. The execution of Stephen was a piece of lynch-law (Acts 7.51ff.). The execution of James took place in the time of King Agrippa I (Acts 12.1ff.). James the brother of the Lord was executed on the urging of the high priest at a time when the procuratorship was temporarily vacant. The Romans disapproved of his action and deprived him of office (*Antt.* 20.9.1, §§197ff.). Elsewhere they in fact seem to have protected the Christians: Paul was saved from an attempt on his life by a Roman officer (Acts 23.12ff.). The decurion Cornelius became a member of the new movement (Acts 10.1ff.). In unruly Palestine the Jesus movement was actually one of the conciliatory, moderate groups. There was no need to persecute it. The Roman authorities came to recognize this fact, however, only after the death of Jesus.

2. Analogies

Even in Acts, the Jesus movement is compared with the movements of Judas and Theudas (Acts 5.36ff.) and had to distinguish itself from other 'Messiahs' and 'prophets' (Matt. 24.24ff.). These analogies call our attention to two different types of radical theocratic movements, prophetic and programmatic. A prophet announces what will be, a programme what should be the case. Prophetic movements are tied to the person of the prophet. Programmatic movements are independent of persons. It is impossible to draw a sharp distinction between the two, but in any event the Jesus movement was a prophetic movement.

(i) In the first century AD, several *prophetic movements* promised a miraculous divine intervention in Israel's favour, a repetition of past acts of salvation: Theudas promised that the Jordan would be divided once again (*Antt.* 20.5.1, §§97ff), while another prophet proclaimed that the miracle at Jericho would be repeated upon the walls of Jerusalem (*Antt.* 20.8.6, §§167ff.). Jonathan promised miracles in the wilderness (*BJ* 7.9.1, §438, cf. also *Antt.* 20.8.6, §§167f.). A Samaritan prophet sought to trace the missing temple vessels to Mount Gerizim (*Antt.* 18.4.1, §§85ff.). Jesus promised a new temple (Mark 14.58). All the prophets led their followers to the place where the miracle was expected. Each time, however, the Romans quickly intervened, inflicted a blood-bath or arrested the leaders. The baptist movement is comparable. John, too, attracted men to the wilderness, taking up the Old Testament promises once again. However, the local ruler Herod Antipas had him executed because he was afraid of a rebellion

(*Antt.* 18.5.2, §118). The New Testament tradition says nothing about this political motive (Mark 6.16ff.).

(ii) The *resistance movement* pursued its aim of a general rebellion against the Romans over a number of generations. It proclaimed the 'sole rule of God' (*BJ* 7.10.1, §410; *Antt.* 18.1.6, §23) and rejected all mortal rulers (*BJ* 2.8.1, §118). This 'sole rule' was imposed through new messiahs: Judas of Galilee, the founder of the movement, in all probability already had his eye on the king-ship (*Antt.* 17.10.5, §§271f.) and handed down his claim to his descendants. One of them, Menahem, appeared in Jerusalem at the beginning of the Jewish war 'in royal dress, like a king' (*BJ* 2.17.8f., §§434, 444) and because of his claim to power was killed by a faction of the city aristocracy which had originally taken his side (*BJ* 2.17.9, §443). God was not, after all, to rule quite 'alone'. This, at any rate, was the view of contemporaries, so that when there was talk of the sole rule of God, of the people, of the law of reason, it was always necessary to ask which social group was using the slogans to support their claims to sole rule. We can also find comparable problems in the Jesus movement. Here too the kingly rule of God was juxtaposed with the expectation of a rule of the Son of man, and no connection was made between them. Here too the specific meaning of the rule of the Son of man was the rule of his followers (Matt. 19.28). Generally speaking, the 'sole rule of God' and the 'kingly rule of God' were comparable, radically theocratic conceptions. Both conceptions arose in Galilee. It could be that Jesus had already come under suspicion from the authorities because of his preaching of the kingdom of God. The disregard of the family is also comparable. True, no one in the Jesus movement wanted to kill friends and relatives for loftier aims (as in *Antt.* 18.23; *BJ* 7.8.1, §266), but it too required hatred of all kindred (Luke 14.26). Both movements were radical, however different they may have been in other respects.

(iii) The *Essenes* were regarded as being peaceable (*BJ* 2.8.6, §135), indeed as pacifists (Philo, *Every Good Man* 12, §76). They came to an arrangement with the rulers (ibid. 13, §§89–91). For example, Herod dispensed with an oath for them (*Antt.* 15.10.4,

§371) and was able to win over one of their prophets as a propagandist for his rule (*Antt.* 15.10.5, §§373ff.). However, this peaceful appearance was deceptive. These remarkable 'pacifists' dreamed of a forthcoming slaughter in which they and the angels of God would massacre the children of darkness (and this included all the foreigners and apostates in the country; cf. the War Scroll 1QM). Unlike the resistance movement, they refrained from imposing the will of God in the present by terrorist means. They therefore looked forward all the more to the great terror at the end of time. Then the 'kingly rule' would finally belong to the God of Israel (1QM 6.6f.). They probably regarded the Jewish rebellion as the great eschatological war. An Essene named John appears in it as a commander of parts of Judaea (*BJ* 2.20.4, §§567). Essenes were cruelly tortured during the war (*BJ* 2.8.10, §§152f.) and the settlement at Qumran was destroyed.

3. Intentions

Opposition to the existing structure of government can be understood only in the light of radical theocratic intentions. All the opposition movements wanted to realize the rule of God consistently or hoped that it would be realized in miraculous fashion. All put forward an explicitly imminent eschatology. Here the imminent end of the old world always also implied the end of Roman rule. And also the end of traditional theocracy. For the new theocracy was not to be introduced by the established mediators but through charismatic leaders and mythical figures.

(i) *Imminent eschatology* Whereas opposition to foreign rule is unmistakable in the eschatology of prophetic movements, resistance fighters and Essenes, such a context played only an indirect part in the case of the Jesus movement. It was so much taken for granted that the kingdom of God which was to dawn in a miraculous way would also bring an end to Roman rule that the fact did not need to be mentioned. Eyes were fixed exclusively on the new world. This new world was not wholly different. Indeed, according to the beliefs of the Jesus movement it already overlapped into this world. An approximate date for it could be given:

it was to come during the lifetime of the first generation (Mark 9.1). It could be located in a particular place: the nations would come streaming in from all points of the compass, to eat with Abraham, Isaac and Jacob (Matt. 8.10f.). Its centre was to lie in Palestine. Moreover, it was a tangible reality. Otherwise it would make no sense to speculate whether people would go into it with one eye or with two (Mark 9.43ff.). Otherwise people would not be able to eat in it (Matt. 8.10f.; Luke 14.15; 22.29f.), drink in it (Mark 14.25) and sit on thrones in it (Matt. 19.28). Nor did it come completely independently of human activity. True, its coming was a miracle. But it also came in miracles, in the exorcisms of Jesus and his followers: 'If it is by the finger of God that I cast out demons, then the kingdom of God has come upon you' (Luke 11.20). However, miracles were possible only if a man had the necessary faith (Mark 11.23). Miracles were required of the wandering charismatics (Matt. 10.8) and regarded as 'possible'. Miraculous healings occupied the same place in the Jesus movement as terrorist actions in the resistance movement. Thus we may not imagine the proclamation of the kingdom of God simply as a theological programme. Its purport was that in the very near future there would be a fundamental change in Palestine, in which a small group of outsiders would become rulers in Israel (Matt. 19.28). This change was heralded by miraculous acts and not by force: the meek would possess the earth, the peacemakers would come into their own (Matt. 5.5,9). Although the Romans were not mentioned, one thing was clear: this would mean the ending of Roman rule and of all earthly government.

(ii) *Messianology* Hopes for the introduction of this new state of affairs were in no way connected with the established priestly aristocracy. New mediators of theocracy had to take their place. In the Jewish War the resistance fighters replaced the compromised high priests by a son of Zadok. Others had hoped that Menahem would be the messianic king. The Essenes wavered between hope for a new high priest and hope for a new king and solved this dilemma by their expectation of two eschatological mediator figures (1QS 9.11); the kingly Messiah was made subordinate to the eschatological priest (1QSa 2.11ff.). Messianic expectations were probably also transferred to Jesus, whether by his disciples (Mark 8.27ff.; Luke 24.21; Acts 1.6), or by other people who were thought to be mad (Mark 1.24; 5.7). Messianic expectations of this kind would be a good reason for the intervention of the aristocracy and the Romans. According to the passion narrative they turned the scales against Jesus (Mark 14.61f.; 15.2; 15.18f., 26f., 32). However, as far as sociological analysis is concerned it would not make much difference if these messianic expectations only arose after Easter. In any event, after Jesus' failure the Jesus movement corrected current conceptions of the Messiah, namely the expectation of an earthly ruler who would surpass David, and replaced them with faith in the crucified and suffering Messiah.

(iii) *'Political ethics'*   The Jesus movement differed most clearly from all comparable radical theocratic movements by virtue of its ethos. Resistance fighters and Essenes demanded hatred of foreigners (cf. 1QS 1.10). This aggressive feature was lacking in the Jesus movement. Whereas other prophetic movements went back to the exodus as a model of liberation from foreign rule, Jesus connected his vision of the future with the sphere of Judaism: the temple building would be the type of what was to come. This is a pointer towards inner renewal. Thus revolt against brutal suppression by the Romans was rejected and transformed into an illustration of the refusal to repent (Luke 13.1ff.). This eirenic undercurrent is unmistakable. The disputed payment of taxes to the Romans is expressly legitimated (Mark 12.13ff.) and the tax officials who work alongside the Romans, those who collected tolls, are accepted (Mark 2.15ff., etc.). Both a tax-collector and a zealot, a resistance fighter (Matt. 10.3; Luke 6.15), are included in the most intimate group of disciples. Members of foreign armies are seen in a positive light (Matt. 8.5ff.; Acts 10.1ff.). All this points to a readiness for reconciliation which transcends frontiers and culminates in the requirement to love one's enemy (Matt. 5.43ff.). The Jesus movement was the peace party among the renewal movements within Judaism. It condemned in the sharpest terms the murder of Zechariah which was arranged by the resistance fighters (*BJ* 4.5.4, §335; Matt. 23.35). Attempts to bring the Jesus movement into close connection with the resistance fighters are absurd: the 'two swords' in Luke 22.38 cannot be taken as a sign of aggressive intentions. At an earlier stage, Luke made the basic rules for wandering charismatics relative to the time after Jesus (Luke 22.35ff.), including the manifest physical helplessness of the wandering preachers. He allowed some means of self-defence. The 'peaceable' Essenes also gave their members weapons against robbers on the road (*BJ* 2.8.4, §125). The saying that Jesus does not bring peace, but a sword, refers to conflict in the family (Luke 12.51ff.).

4. Causes

The radical theocratic movements arose out of the crisis over theocracy. The Jesus movement, too, was connected with the socio-political tensions in Palestine. Its proclamation of the imminence of the kingdom of God could only find a ready echo in a country in which no satisfactory solution had been found to the problem of government. Outside Palestine, in the earliest Hellenistic Christianity, the kingdom of God almost ceased to be mentioned. Paul's use of the term is only marginal (e.g. Rom. 14.17; I Cor. 4.20). The society in which he lived lacked the deep-rooted political tensions in the context of which he had once been brought up and educated. Generally speaking, these tensions may be derived from the conflict between native and alien structures of rule. Theocracy and monarchy could be associated with the traditions of Israel; the empire and the city states were alien to it. Herod's attempt to create a permanent equilibrium on the foundation of a Hellenistic monarchy remained unsuccessful. Friction between the varied structures of government above all weakened the idea of theocracy and thus gave rise to dreams of this theocracy in a radical form. Finally, the social and political tensions got out of hand and led to the Jewish war.[21]

(1) *The Roman empire* After 63 BC Palestine was part of the Roman empire. Any survey of the first century of Roman policy in Palestine must find fault with it for contributing to the instability of the situation by changes of direction and an inadequate

presence in both the political and the military spheres.

(*a*) The Romans fluctuated between centralized and decentralized, direct and indirect rule. Pompey divided up Palestine between the Hellenistic city states which he had liberated from Jewish rule (*Antt.* 14.4.3, §§74ff.). The Jewish high priests and ethnarchs were confined to Jewish territory. Gabinius sub-divided it further into five administrative areas and thus weakened the influence of the Jewish ethnarchs in Jerusalem even more (*Antt.* 14.6.4, §91). However, he did succeed in exploiting conflicts in the Roman Civil War in his own interest. Caesar again confirmed his position as ethnarch over the whole of Judaea. Herod was even appointed as its king (40 BC). His success in driving out the Parthians and bringing peace to the country was rewarded by extensions to his territory. Whereas decentralization had been the policy even at the end of the republic, under Augustus there was a return to centralization, but it was not permanent. After the death of Herod, his land was divided up among his sons. After only ten years, the chief heirs were deposed, and within his territory, in Judaea and Samaria, there was a change from indirect to direct rule. In the more marginal areas, however, Herodian princes continued to rule and dreamed of a restoration of the Herodian dynasty. Agrippa (AD 41–44) had success for a short time: he ruled over an area which was comparable in extent to Herod's kingdom. However, after his death the Romans again took over direct responsibility for government in Judaea. This to-ing and fro-ing had an unsettling effect. It was impossible for any form of government to develop which was legitimated by a long period of power and tradition. They experimented with client rulers, or with the aristocracy; divisions were first made and then unmade. No institution was given a chance of becoming powerful enough to be able to control the difficult territory. Palestine lived in a constant state of constitutional crisis.

(*b*) Since the Romans did not allow the rise of a strong native aristocracy, they should have maintained an authoritative presence themselves. But they had the country administered by a subordinate prefect or procurator whose political influence was quite weak. He was subject to three forms of control. First of all

were the Herodian petty princes, who did not allow any opportunity of demonstrating the weakness of their rival to go by. For
example, when Pilate had shields hung up in his buildings in
Jerusalem with the imperial inscription on them, the Herodians
appeared at the head of those who protested against them (Philo,
Leg. ad Gaium 38, §300), although Antipas had even put up
statues in his palace in Tiberias (Josephus, *Vita* 12, 65). Tensions
between Pilate and Antipas (as in Luke 23.12) were inevitable.
Secondly, the prefect of Judaea was under the control of the
legate of Syria, on whose legions he relied in times of crisis. The
population also went to the legate with their complaints. Thus
Pilate was deposed by the legate after taking action against an
armed prophetic movement among the Samaritans (*Antt.* 18.4.2,
§§88ff.). How insecure he must have been in his position, if he
was not even allowed to do that! The emperor was the third and
the supreme authority. After petitions from the Jews, even the
procurators were sometimes overruled. Their orders could be
rescinded (*Antt.* 20.1.1, §§6ff.; Philo, *Leg. ad Gaium* 38, §§303ff.).
One of them was even deposed (*Antt.* 20.6.3, §§134ff.). So the
procurator had to tread carefully. John 19.12 is right in indicating
that Pilate could be blackmailed by the threat of a complaint to
Caesar. The only way another procurator knew of protecting
himself against criticism from the high priest was to have him
done away with by an assassin – which is certainly not a sign of
political strength (*Antt.* 20.8.5, §§162ff.).

(*c*) The Romans maintained only a small military presence. It
was only after the Bar-Kochba revolt that they stationed a legion
in the plain of Megiddo. Before that there had only been three
thousand men in Caesarea, and a cohort in Jerusalem. The troops
were not of the best quality. The soldiers were recruited from the
Hellenistic city states and shared their fanatical hatred of the
Jews. This led to unnecessary friction. For example, one soldier
burnt a scroll of the Torah (*BJ* 2.12.2, §229); another uncovered
his bottom in public during the Passover and farted (*BJ* 2.12.1,
§224). After the death of Agrippa I, in Caesarea and Sebaste
soldiers dragged statues of his daughters into the brothels, as an
insult to a king who had been well-disposed towards the Jews
(*Antt.* 19.9.1, §357). These soldiers with their anti-Jewish attitude

were the most unsuited force imaginable for keeping the land
under effective control. The emperor sensibly ordered that they
should be exchanged for other troops, but this command was
never carried out (*Antt.* 19.9.2, §§365f.). By contrast, higher ranks
in the Roman army were better disposed towards the Jews. Thus
during clashes between Gentiles and Jews in Caesarea the troops
took the side of the Gentiles, whereas their officers sought to
mediate between the opposing factions (*BJ* 2.13.7, §§266ff.). Like
Cornelius, the centurion of Caesarea, the centurion of Capernaum
sympathized with the Jews (Luke 7.1ff.; Acts 10.1ff.). The differ-
ing attitude to the Jews within the military hierarchy is particularly evident in the passion narrative: the common soldiers
mock Jesus as 'king of the Jews' (Mark 15.16ff.), whereas a centurion recognizes in him the 'Son of God' (Mark 15.39).

(ii) *Hellenistic city states*   These were to be found only rarely in
Jewish Palestine.[22] True, Josephus calls Jerusalem a *polis*, but it
did not have the corresponding civic institutions. From the time
of Alexander onwards, the growth of city states is a characteristic
of constitutional history throughout the Near East. More and
more cities were governed by an assembly of all the citizens (the
ecclesia), and a group of magistrates elected by it (the *boule*); as a
sign of its communal autonomy, each city state would mint its
own coinage. City states of this kind were thickly clustered
around Jewish territory. On the Mediterranean there were Sidon,
Tyre, Ptolemais, Dor, Ashkelon, Gaza and Raphia. In
Transjordania, Scythopolis, Hippos, Gadara, Philadelphia and
other cities had combined to form the Decapolis. In the second
century BC a Hellenistic reform attempt to add Jerusalem to the
economic and cultural network of these city states had come to
grief on the opposition of the conservative country-dwellers.[23]
The backlash from this led to the discrediting of the idea of the
polis and – during the course of the Maccabean policy of expan-
sion – to the subjection of the surrounding city states, with the
exception of Ashkelon. Consequently in 63 BC Pompey could
appear as the liberator of the cities from the Jewish yoke. In
Palestine, as elsewhere, the Romans attempted to encourage the
communal institutions that were familiar to them and to divide

the country up into city states. Only where these were too weak and conditions were too backward did they prefer to have a people disciplined by native client princes. Attempts made by Gabinius to prepare for a decentralized form of government based on local communities in Palestine remained unsuccessful. Only the Herods continued Roman policy by founding a number of cities with the constitution of a *polis*; however, they had no hesitation in interfering in their government. Significantly, these were in border areas like Caesarea (*BJ* 2.14.4, §284), Sebaste (*Antt.* 15.8.5, §§292ff.) and Caesarea Philippi (*Vita* 13, §74). The Gentile element was dominant in them. In general, Jews and Gentiles found it very difficult to live together in these cities. From being the former masters of the country, the Jews had become small minorities. In Caesarea, the experiment of letting the two groups live side by side with equal rights proved a failure. The inhabitants had constant disputes over civic rights until Nero promised them to the Greeks (*Antt.* 20.8.9, §§182ff.; *BJ* 2.14.4, §284). At the beginning of the Jewish war there were pogroms in almost all the neighbouring city states: in Caesarea, Scythopolis, Ashkelon, Ptolemais, Tyre, Hippos, Gadara and Damascus (*BJ* 2.17.10, §456; 2.18.3, 5, §§466ff., 477f.; 2.20.2, §§559ff.) In Tiberias, on the other hand, the Gentile minority was massacred (*Vita* 12, §67). In cities which were further away from Jewish territory and which therefore had less to fear from the claims of the Jewish nationalists to home rule, e.g. in Antioch, Sidon and Apamea, there were no attacks on the Jews (*BJ* 2.18.5, §479). The gulf between Judaism and the city states and their institutions is clear enough. The Jews were against the new forms on religious grounds alone: they would have made it possible for Jews and Gentiles to live together. Foreigners would have become fellow-citizens, and Jews 'foreigners'. The Gentile gymnasia would have led to a liberalization in culture, and the rise of a number of autonomous centres would have weakened the position of Jerusalem. Attempts at assimilation like those in Alexandrian Judaism cannot be found in Palestine. In general, the Jews kept their distance from the city states. This is also true of the Jesus movement (see ch.VI.1, pp. 47f. above). It is all the more remarkable that its local communities took over the term *ecclesia* from the constitution of the city state to denote their own assemblies, even where they drew lines of demarcation over against the Gentiles (Matt. 18.15ff.; 16.18).[24] This is another indication that in the Jesus movement the hard and fast lines between Gentiles and Jews were being broken down.

(iii) *The Jewish aristocracy* The Jews did not form a *polis* but an *ethnos*, with the high priest and the Sanhedrin at its head. The aristocracy were the natural allies of the Romans, because their members were 'peace-loving men, simply out of concern for their possessions' (*BJ* 2.16.2, §338). This makes it all the more serious that the Romans tolerated the weakening of aristocratic institutions and themselves helped on the process.

(*a*) In principle, the office of high priest was hereditary and lasted for life. However, even the Hasmonean dynasty was not a legitimate one. True, to begin with, Herod appointed a son of Zadok, but he then replaced high priests at his own discretion, so that the office also ceased to have its character as a position for life. Again, Herod was taken to task by the Romans for the murder of a high priest, but he was excused with the assurance that a king was free to exercise his power (*Antt.* 15.3.8, §76). Thus the Romans tolerated the devaluation of the office of high priest under Herod. Not only that: they continued his practice of replacing the high priest at will. Between AD 6 and AD 66 there were eighteen high priests, of whom only three ruled for more than two years, namely Annas (AD 6–15), Caiaphas (AD 18–36) and Ananias (AD 47–59). Unfortunately we have only fragmentary information about the reasons for the countless depositions: the high priest Jonathan criticized the procurator's administration and therefore was done away with (*Antt.* 20.8.5, §§162ff.); Ananias the son of Nedebaius was brought to Rome in chains along with a rebel (*Antt.* 20.6.2, §131). There can be no question of collaboration here. The office of high priest was obviously drawn into conflicts with the Romans.[25] Simony and intrigue diminished its reputation. It is understandable that the resistance fighters removed the established high priestly families from power and again chose a son of Zadok as high priest (*BJ* 4.3.8, §§155ff.).

(*b*) The Sanhedrin consisted of three groups: the high priests, the elders and the scribes (Mark 15.1). The high priests were the aristocracy of worship, the elders the aristocracy of the rich, and the scribes the aristocracy of the educated. The first two groups had protected themselves against competitors by dynastic or economic privileges. Only through education in law and religion could new groups enter the Sanhedrin. Here we can see a clear instance of the circulation of *élites*. By means of the Sanhedrin, the Pharisees,[26] or their scribes, developed in the course of a century from being a rebellious opposition which had involved the country in a bloody civil war as early as the time of Alexander Jannaeus (103–76 BC) to becoming the only representatives of Judaism after AD 70. In achieving this they excluded not only their opponents, the Sadducean aristocracy, but also all rival renewal movements. Their rise was furthered by conflicts between secular and spiritual power. The Pharisees argued that the two should be separated. They therefore found support among the political forces who were inevitably interested in the absence of the priestly aristocracy from politics. The successor of Alexander Jannaeus, being a woman, could not become high priest. Weak high priests, who refrained from politics, were in her interest. Under her, Pharisees were accepted into the Sanhedrin. Herod too could not become high priest since he was a layman and an Idumaean. So he had to devalue the office. He decimated the Sadducean aristocracy from whom the high priests were drawn, by assassination (*Antt.* 15.1.2, §6; 14.9.4, §175), but treated the Pharisaic movement very kindly (*Antt.* 15.1.1, §§3f.; 15.10.4, §370). Under direct Roman rule the Pharisees must have achieved further influence over the Sanhedrin. Josephus is probably describing conditions in his own time when he reports that the Pharisees had such a strong position among the people that the Sadducees had to show respect to them in public (*Antt.* 18.1.4, §17). The great hour for Pharisaism struck after the catastrophe of AD 70. In Jamnia the Hillelites, their moderate wing, formed a new Sanhedrin, reconstituted Judaism and excluded all competing renewal movements. The Christians, too, were excommunicated.

(*c*) There were tensions between the Jesus movement and the aristocracy of the temple state who were primarily responsible for the execution of Jesus (Mark 11.18; 12.12; 14.1). Their concern over the new movement is understandable when we think of its critical attitude over the temple: the cleansing of the temple (Mark 11.15), the merely relative position accorded to the temple in connection with reconciliation and oaths (Matt. 5.23f., 33ff.; 23.16ff.), and the prophecies about the temple (Mark 14.58f.; Acts 6.14; Matt. 23.28). Anyone who accorded a relative and not an absolute position to the temple and the law was attacking the privileges of the priestly aristocracy. It is therefore probable that the Sanhedrin were the prime movers in the persecution of the Jesus movement (Acts 4.5ff.; 5.17ff.; 6.15; *Antt.* 20.9.1, §§197ff.). We must see these tensions as being the reason why in the course of tradition the passion narrative attaches more blame to the Jewish authorities than it does to the Romans. Here we have more than a tendency to exonerate the Romans. It reflected the experiences of the Jesus movement.

(iv) *The Herodian monarchy*   Even this was incapable of guaranteeing a permanent order for Palestine.[27] True, Herod succeeded in keeping it under control for thirty-four years (37–4 BC). But he simply suppressed existing tensions, which were unleashed all the more explosively after his death. His successor Archelaus had to be removed in AD 6 because he was unable to get on with the aristocracy. Again, during his short reign Agrippa I (AD 41–44) had success with his Jewish subjects, but he failed with the Hellenistic parts of the population. The causes of the failure of the dynasty of the Herods were their marked lack of credentials, their policy of repressing rival centres of power, a propaganda which inevitably violated religious feelings, and the lack of homogeneity among the population.

(a) Lack of credentials. Even the Hasmoneans had been usurpers. But they had achieved national independence and had subsequently legitimated their rule by means of a state treaty with the Jewish people (I Macc. 14.27ff.). Their attempt nevertheless to transform the Jewish ethnarchy into an absolute monarchy along Hellenistic lines came up against resistance. Under Alexander Jannaeus (103–76 BC) there was a six-year civil war. When Pompey reorganized affairs in Palestine he was visited by a popular delegation which argued for a restoration of priestly rule

(*Antt.* 14.3.2, §41; Diodorus Siculus XL.2). If the Hasmoneans already had difficulties in establishing a Hellenistic monarchy, this was even more the case with Herod. His credentials were minimal. He owed his kingship to a decree of the Roman Senate and not to any Jewish authority. He did not come forward as an advocate of national independence but as its liquidator. He was not descended from any royal dynasty, but first had to remove from the scene by murder a dynasty which was taken to be legitimate. He was not even a proper Jew, but an Idumaean. His appointment as king was a brilliant blunder on the part of the Romans. They burdened the land with a dynasty which had no dynastic legitimation and thus contradicted their own principles, for which they were justly critized by the last Hasmonean king (*Antt.* 14.15.2, §§403ff.). Only the shock of the Parthian invasion makes the Roman error comprehensible: they handed over to Herod a country which was bound to be seized. His claim to rule was based on military conquest. His kingdom continued the absolutist rule of Hellenistic mercenary leaders and was utterly different from a popular kingdom of the Israelite kind. It went against the traditions of the country. So there was nothing left for him but to compensate for his lack of legitimation by a combination of repression and propaganda.

(*b*) Herod's policy of repression was directed against all rival centres of power, and not so much against ordinary people. First of all, Herod had to fear the Hasmonean dynasty, although he was allied to it through marriage. In a coolly calculated programme of murder he exterminated his wife's family. Even she herself and her children were to become his victims. The story of the massacre of the innocents in Bethlehem is a popular echo of these events (Matt. 2.7ff.). Secondly, he had to eliminate the aristocracy. He compromised the office of high priest by frequently changing its holder. He even appointed diaspora Jews (*Antt.* 15.2.4, §22; 15.9.3, §§320ff.) in order to create a counterweight against the old established Jerusalem families. He also locked up the high priestly robes and only allowed them to be used at festivals (*Antt.* 15.11.4, §§403ff.). The Sanhedrin, too, was intimidated by murders and its authority was limited. Herod maintained a secret service to keep down the opposition (*Antt.* 15.10.3,

§366), and demoralized the aristocracy by terror and by confiscations (*Antt.* 17.11.2, §307). In this way he acted against the classes and institutions which were important for the peace of the country. Perhaps he did so deliberately. Herod wanted no guarantors of order apart from himself. He had to show the Romans that he was the only one who could bring about order. So he made chaos the alternative to his reign, and when he died, chaos broke out. Since another delegation appeared before Augustus at the same time, arguing that the monarchy should be abolished and that Palestine should be attached to the province of Syria, the Romans must have got the message (*Antt.* 17.11.2, §§304ff., 314). They gave to Herod's successor Archelaus, who also happened to be in Rome, the task of paying closer attention to the wishes expressed by the delegation (*Antt.* 17.13.2, §342). Because he failed to do this he was deposed after a ten-year rule. These events have been echoed by the synoptic tradition: according to Luke 19.12ff. a nobleman travels to a distant country to get himself a kingdom. However, his fellow-citizens send a delegation which argues against his being made king. It is interesting that the rebellious citizens are condemned in the parable. Were the Herods more popular among the people than with the aristocracy?

(*c*) Herod's propaganda could be based on tangible success. After the confusion of the civil wars, Herod had extended the *pax Romana* to Palestine. The country had an economic revival. The development of new territory and a heavy programme of building are evidence of this. Herod impressed his Gentile subjects with new institutions and festivals. Here he transgressed the commandment against making images (*Antt.* 15.9.5, §§327ff.) and went against Jewish monotheism; he had himself celebrated as god (*OGIS* 415). He had to be more careful with his Jewish subjects. He succeeded in finding a prophet who promised him the kingdom in God's name (*Antt.* 15.10.5, §§373ff.). He probably also wanted to promote himself as Messiah, the new David. Whereas David had only made preparations for building the temple, and Solomon had carried them out, Herod did both (*Antt.* 15.11.1, §§380ff.) Was he not greater even than David? Thus Herod usurped not only power, but the messianic hopes of

Israel. This must have had a devastating effect and aroused even greater longing for the true Messiah, who would not hand the Jewish people over to the power of Rome, but would hand over power to the Jewish people. This longing must have increased during Herod's long reign. After his death, messianic pretenders appeared everywhere: Judas in Galilee, Simon in Peraea, Athronges in Judaea (*Antt.* 17.10.5–7, §§271ff.). 'Such madness seized the nation at that time because they had no king of their own . . .' (*Antt.* 17.10.6, §277). We must therefore suppose that this messianic hope continued to flourish in the country for a long time to come.[28] It is probable that Jesus also came up against it. The Jesus movement declared such notions to be erroneous. Anyone who expressed them must be mad: a demon must have seized his mind (Mark 1.24; 5.7; 8.29ff.; Matt. 4.8ff.). But one must not simply think in terms of demons. Ideas like this were produced by the political situation. And we cannot rule out the possibility that men affected in this way were particularly sensitive to ideas that were in the air. We may, for example, recall the mad prophets of disaster who prophesied the fall of Jerusalem before the Jewish war (*BJ* 6.5.3, §§300ff.).

(*d*) The Romans expected that the Herods would integrate Judaea into the Roman empire. They therefore transferred to him areas where Jews and Gentiles had to live together. Herod I attempted to do justice to both sections of the population, but compromised himself with the Jews by his assimilation to Gentile customs (e.g. *Antt.* 15.8.1, §§267ff.). Agrippa I was particularly well-disposed to the Jews (cf. Acts 12.3; *Antt.* 19.7.3f., §§330ff.), but kept a tight grip on the Gentiles. Thus for example he waged an economic war against the Hellenistic cities of Tyre and Sidon (Acts 12.20ff.). His acclamation as 'god' in Caesarea (*Antt.* 19.8.2, §§343ff.; Acts 12.21ff.) surely did not arise out of any honest respect. On the contrary, the acclamation was intended to compromise him with his Jewish subjects. The true feelings of the people of Caesarea in fact emerged after his death: they held feasts in celebration and mocked the dead man by having statues of his daughters put up on the roofs of brothels (*Antt.* 19.9.1, §357). The Jews interpreted his death as a punishment for the tolerant acceptance of blasphemy, the Christians as a punishment for his persecution of them (Acts 12.1ff.). The historian, however, will see the events at his death above all as an illustration of how hard it was to integrate Jews and Gentiles. Was this perhaps one reason why the Romans abandoned the experiment of a Herodian dynasty in Palestine? After the death of Agrippa I the country was again put under a procurator. Generally speaking, the policy of integration attempted by Romans and the Herods came to grief. The lack of homogeneity in the population was too great.

5. Summary

Palestine was in a constant state of crisis. It proved impossible to achieve a permanent balance between the various structures of government. In political terms, the powers of the aristocracy, who were concerned for an equilibrium, were weakened by friction with the Herodian client rulers and the Roman procurators. They were compromised, and thus lost their ideological force as representatives of the theocracy. The crisis over theocracy was the breeding-ground for radical theocratic movements. Tensions between earthly structures of government furthered the longing for the kingdom of God. The synoptic tradition illustrates this situation in the saying about the kingdom divided against itself, which is unable to stand (Mark 3.24f.). Here the end of the rule of Satan signalizes the beginning of the rule of God. We may understand the kingdom of Satan as a symbolic accentuation of the negative experiences of earthly rule. According to the apocalypse of the shepherds in Ethiopic Enoch 85–90, when Israel lost its political independence, God delegated rule over it to the fallen angels, the subjects of Satan. The mythological events here reflect political ones. In a different way, this sort of situation can be detected from the synoptic apocalypse. The intention of the Roman emperor Gaius to desecrate the Jerusalem temple by putting up a statue of himself in it (Mark 13.14ff.) is seen as the beginning of the great eschatological tribulation. Hope for the Son of man is intensified by political subjection. In my view, therefore, there is good reason for assuming that the radical theocratic dream of the kingdom of God should be taken in close connection with the socio-political tensions in Palestine. Beyond question, however, it also points beyond this historical situation.

VIII. Socio-cultural Factors

1. The phenomenon

In most renewal movements within Judaism, a stricter interpretation of the Torah was bound up with the imminent expectation of the kingdom of God. If we can find connections between socio-political tensions and this imminent expectation, in the case of the stricter interpretation of the Torah we find an offshoot of the socio-cultural tensions between Jewish and Hellenistic culture. The Torah gave Judaism its identity, defined its privileged and perilous position among the nations and gave it its self-awareness. Discussion of the true Torah and its interpretation points to a crisis of identity within Judaism. Its role among the nations had become problematical. There was uncertainty (often subconsciously) over which was the better course to follow: assimilation or detachment; criticism or approval and further development; stricter interpretation of the Torah or laxer interpretation. The same was true of the Jesus movement. Here there was a basic affirmation of the law. But it was interpreted with an eye to the 'others' – in those very places where there was a fundamental recognition of it. For the encounter with Hellenistic education and its philosophical colouring created a desire to derive the manifold variety of the law from a few basic principles: love of God and of one's neighbour (Mark 12.28ff.; Test. XII Patr., e.g. Iss. 5.2; Benj. 3.3, etc.), or the 'golden rule' (e.g. Matt. 7.12; Sir. 34.15). In this way, people thought themselves the equals of Hellenism. The 'golden rule' comes from popular philosophy; among the Greeks, too, piety and righteousness were regarded as the most important dimensions of ethical conduct (cf. Xenophon,

Mem. 4.8.11). Any good elements that were to be found among others could be incorporated into native traditions. Furthermore, if people interpreted the Torah more strictly, they felt themselves to be superior to the rest.[29]

(i) *Intensification of norms*   In the case of norms, a distinction must be drawn between action and motivation. One can ask 'What should be done?' and 'Why should it be done?' In the Jesus movement, we can see a more radical attitude to traditional norms in the case of both these aspects. The action required is made more difficult, and the requirement is also extended to the inner motivation behind the action. A table should make this situation clear:

Sphere of norms	Action	Motivation
Aggression	Not only aggressive behaviour is forbidden but even defence against aggression (Matt. 5.39ff.).	Not only aggressive actions are forbidden, but even anger within (Matt. 5.21ff.) and sublimated forms of aggression like moralizing (Matt. 7.1ff.).
Sexuality	Even divorce and marriage to a separated woman comprise adultery (Mark 10.2ff.).	Adultery begins with sexual stimulation and erotic fascination (Matt. 5.27f.).
Communication	Every word should be as true as if it were given on oath. Consequently oaths are forbidden (Matt. 5.34ff.).	The decisive thing is not what is said, but a man's inward attitude (Matt. 12.34).
Possessions	Radical discipleship calls for radical renunciation of possessions (Mark 10.17ff.).	In the last resort, what is required is inner freedom from possessions, and freedom towards providence (Matt. 6.25).

In this context it is interesting that there are parallels in Hellenism for radical attitudes over motivation. Cleanthes had long ago asserted that anyone who entertains a desire will perform the corresponding action when opportunity presents itself (frag.

573). Similar notions also penetrated Judaism from popular philosophy, with the result that the Decalogue could be summed up in the commandment 'You shall not covet' (Rom. 7.7; 13.9).

(ii) *Relaxation of norms* The ethos of the synoptic tradition is characterized by the intertwining of two tendencies: the intensification of norms and their relaxation. While those interpretations of the law which intensified its norms were to be found above all in the social sphere, it is in the religious sphere that we find interpretations which relax these norms. People had a 'liberal' attitude towards the prohibition against images. The representation of the emperor was accepted on coins (Mark 12.13ff.). People had a 'liberal' attitude towards the rules for the sabbath (Mark 2.27 etc.), towards separation from Gentiles and sinners and the demands for purity which were connected with it (Mark 7.15). As a result, restrictions in communication between Jews and Gentiles were made merely relative. It is therefore no coincidence that we find comparable 'liberal' views in Hellenistic Judaism, where there was daily contact with the problem of communication between Jews and Gentiles. Ps.Phocylides also affirms that only the soul makes the body pure (28). Pictures were to be found in diaspora synagogues (cf. Dura Europus). We find a spiritualization of ritual commandments in the allegories of Alexandrian Judaism.

(iii) *The connection between the intensification of norms and their relaxation* may be interpreted in various ways. In that the intensification of norms and their relaxation belong to different spheres, one could say that, for the Jesus movement, obligations between one man and another are more important than religious duties. As a result, the latter are relaxed and the former are made relative. However, this interpretation fails when the same norms are both intensified and relaxed, when the intensification of norms dialectically becomes the relaxation of norms. This inversion is consistent. If it becomes clear that everyone must inevitably fall short of the intensified norms, all moral self-righteousness must appear to be hypocrisy. If adultery begins by being attracted erotically by another woman, who would have the

right to cast the first stone in the case of manifest adultery? If
anger and murder are on the same level, who could fail to recognize his own impulses in the crime? Must not even a man's
enemy appear as his brother? Can one still make a neat distinction
between the good man and the evil man where God makes his
sun rise on both (Matt. 5.45)? Is it not a misunderstanding of the
significance of ethical norms to use them as a means of moral
aggression? We can see in the Jesus movement the dawning of the
tremendous insight that human social life is more than a matter of
morality.

2. Analogies

There were numerous analogies in the Judaism of the time to this
intensification of norms. All the renewal movements wanted the
Torah to be observed more consistently than before. All were
concerned for a new formulation of Jewish identity, i.e. for all
those characteristics and modes of behaviour which could be seen
to be specifically Jewish and which marked the difference between
Jews and Gentiles.

(i) *The resistance movement*   Unlike the Jesus movement, the resistance movement intensified the religious commandments and
relaxed the social commandments. Great stress was laid above all
on the first commandment. The sole rule of God stood at the
centre of the programme of the zealots (*BJ* 2.8.1, §118; 7.10.1,
§§410, 418f.; *Antt.* 18.1.6, §23). The prohibition against making
images was observed with fanatical seriousness. It was forbidden
to make, look at, touch or carry images. Coins were tabu. So too
were the Hellenistic cities, in which one would inevitably come
upon images of the gods (Hippolytus, *Adv.haer.* 9.26). The commandment to practise circumcision was also observed fanatically.
Uncircumcised Jews were kidnapped and given the alternative
of execution as lawbreakers or observing the law (*Adv.haer.*
9.26). On the other hand, fundamental social laws, e.g. the commandment to honour one's parents, were broken. In the Jewish
war, deserters were killed and left unburied. Members of the
movement who wanted to bury their relatives were themselves

executed and left unburied (*BJ* 4.6.2, §§381ff.; cf. Matt. 8.21f.). It was impossible to avoid the commandment against killing. The prohibition against slavery was disregarded: hostages were taken to force the release of imprisoned fellow-members (*Antt.* 20.9.3, §§208ff.). False accusations were used to get 'collaborators' out of the way (*BJ* 5.10.4, §§439ff.). Certainly the resistance fighters had a vision of an Israel with more social justice. The social commandments were taken seriously. The Decalogue was taken to apply to the whole nation. However, the resistance fighters determined who belonged to the nation. They excluded the rich, treating them as if there were 'no difference between them and foreigners, as they were thought to have betrayed the freedom won by the Jews at such cost and avowedly to have chosen servitude to Rome' (*BJ* 7.8.1, §255).

(ii) *The Essenes* They interpreted the Torah strictly in both the religious and the social spheres. In the religious sphere, their concern for priestly purity is striking. Because the temple in Jerusalem had been 'defiled', in the second century BC they had cut themselves off from it. They sought to realize their ideal of purity in the wilderness (CD 3.20–4.19). It was an internalized ideal of purity, since they were aware that external rites are no guarantee of purity (1QS 3.4ff.). However, they were afraid of being infected by impurity (1QS 6.16ff.; 7.19f.), which is why they clearly shrank from contact with the world (1QS 5.10ff.). The preservation of priestly holiness also involved an extreme observance of the laws for the sabbath. Thus while the rabbis allowed, for example, the rescue of an animal which had fallen into a well on the sabbath (b.Shab.128b; Matt. 12.11), this was forbidden by the Essenes (CD 11.13f.). We also find intensification of the norms in the case of the central areas of behaviour between one man and another: aggression, sexuality, communication and possessions. However, these intensifications were related primarily to fellow-members of the community. Aggression against other members was strictly forbidden. Losing one's temper was punished by a year's exclusion from the community (1QS 6.26f.; 7.2). However, there was an injunction to hate all men outside the community (1QS 1.10; 9.21ff.). A rigorous attitude was maintained in sexual matters. The nucleus of the Essenes lived a celibate life (*BJ* 2.8.2, §120); others regarded sexual activity as legitimate only for the purpose of continuing the group (*BJ* 2.8.13, §§160f.). There were also strict rules about speaking. For example, the punishment for a foolish remark was three months' exclusion from the community (1QS 7.9). The rule was that there should be unqualified openness towards members of the community, but strict silence towards all the rest (*BJ* 2.8.7, §141; 1QS 5.15f.). Oaths were repudiated on principle (*BJ* 2.8.6, §§135f.). However, it was the radical Essene attitude towards possessions which attracted the most attention, even in antiquity. There were no private possessions in the community (*BJ* 2.8.3, §122; *Antt.* 18.1.5, §20; Philo, *Every Good Man* 12, §86). After one year's probation, new members handed over their possessions and their wages to the community (1QS 6.19ff.). False information about possessions led to severe punishment (1QS 6.25). And whereas they described themselves as the 'poor' chosen by God (1QpHab 12.3,6,10), they condemned the quest for possessions as a characteristic of the sinful world (1QS 10.19; 11.2; 1QpHab.6.1; 8.10f.).

(iii) *The Pharisees* They are comparable with the Essenes in that they made a wide-ranging interpretation of the requirements for priestly purity and also extended them to the laity. However, whereas the Essenes put the intensified norms into practice in abrupt separation from society, the Pharisees attempted to practise them in normal everyday life. This tendency to adapt the law to the wide variety of everyday situations was in accordance with the social context of Pharisaism. It was the only renewal movement within Judaism which was not involved with an eccentric form of living. It sought to put the Torah to effect in normal life. The requirement of a tithe was extended consistently to all agricultural products (Matt. 23.23) and the demand for purity was interpreted in a reasonable way: one can hardly object to washing hands (Mark 7.3f.) and clean household utensils (Matt. 23.23). Christian polemic is not very convincing here. The law about the sabbath was given a strict but practicable form: it was permissible to help men and animals in distress (Matt. 12.11f.; b.Shab 128b; b.Yoma 84b). The Pharisaic attempt to make rules for all areas of everyday life and to legitimate their programme by the Torah deserves respect – not least because it is an attempt to do two contradictory things: on the one hand to intensify the norms, and on the other to adapt them to normal life. From an outsider's point of view, this inner contradiction must inevitably lead to the charge of hypocrisy. Alexander Jannaeus (103–77 BC) already warned against the 'hypocrites who imitate the Pharisees' (b.Sota 22b). The Jesus movement pilloried the contradictions between teaching and conduct (Matt. 23.3ff.). The Essenes objected that they (i.e. the community of the man of lies) would whitewash the wall round the law (CD 19.24ff.), 'seek smooth things' (CD 1.18f.) and only pretend observance of the Torah. For the radical movements, Pharisaism, with its contrived compromises, was not consistent enough. It was easy from the periphery of society to criticize a group which had a serious concern for 'true living' within the context of a given society. On the whole, the Pharisees themselves saw the contradiction between their intensification of the norms and their adaptation of them. The result was that in the first century AD they split into two schools: the school of the stricter Shammai and that of the more 'liberal' Hillel. The Shammaites represented the concern for the intensification of norms, the Hillelites that for practicability. Thus the Shammaites required strict separation from the Gentiles. In eighteen halachoth, there were prohibitions against various Gentile foods, the Greek language, Gentile testimony, Gentile gifts, sons and daughters-in-law (j.Shab.3c 49ff.). They even used force against the Hillelites to carry through these intensified norms (j.Shab.3c 34ff.). Only after the catastrophe of AD 70 did the more moderate Hillelites succeed in gaining the upper hand.

3. Intentions

We find tendencies to intensify norms throughout Judaism. Even the conservative Sadduccees wanted to apply the law strictly (*Antt.* 20.9.1, §199). By contrast, liberalizing tendencies are rare. It is therefore the phenomenon of the rigorist interpretation of the law above all that calls for sociological explanation (according to the methodological maxim that whatever is found to be wide-spread in society is determined by social causes). First indications of the social determination of the intensification of norms give explicit reasons for interpretations which intensify norms. Two tendencies towards social segregation emerge clearly here: tendencies towards inter-cultural segregation from the Gentiles, and tendencies towards intra-cultural segregation from other Jewish groups. The two belong together dialectically.

(i) Many renewal movements pursued the aim of *inter-cultural segregation* by means of interpretations of their own culture in which norms were intensified. This was clearest in the case of the Jewish resistance fighters in the first century AD. The radical interpretation of the first commandment was *a priori* aimed against foreigners. If God was the sole lord, then no other lords could be recognized. It was therefore said that the Jews 'should not think that the Romans were stronger than they were themselves, but rather should recognize God as their only lord' (*BJ* 7.10.1, §410). With their eighteen halachoth which intensified the norms of the Torah, the Shammaites pressed for strict separation. Even the Jesus movement sometimes gave separatist tendencies as their reason for intensifying the demands of the law. This was the motive behind the commandment to love one's enemy: 'If you salute only your brethren, what more are you doing than others? Do not even the Gentiles do the same?' (Matt. 5.47). The same is true of the demand not to worry about food, drink and clothing. Here, too, it is said that the Gentiles seek all these things (Matt. 6.37). The Lord's Prayer is used in the awareness that it is different from the empty phrases of the Gentiles (Matt. 6.7). Or the activity of the wandering charismatics is limited to Israel (Matt. 10.5f.). Of course such tendencies towards inter-cultural segregation are rare. Only a few of the instructions for conduct which intensify the norms of the law are motivated in this way. Here it should be remembered that the more strictly the norms of a society are defined, the fewer people can observe them. The stricter the demands on the 'true Jews', the smaller the group of 'true Jews' becomes. Segregation from others is thus transferred to within the culture. Parts of the former inner group become outsiders. Inter-cultural segregation becomes intra-cultural.

(ii) *Tendencies towards intra-cultural differentiation* emerge with an intrinsic necessity from attempts at inter-cultural segregation, when there are a number of rival renewal movements. In Palestine, every renewal movement wanted to make the better Israel a reality. Each of them had to demote the other Jews to the status of Israelites of the second rank, or even equate them with the Gentiles. Thus the attempt to preserve the identity of the people over against superior alien cultures paradoxically led to the loss of this identity. Now there were several groups, all of which claimed to be the true Israel.

(*a*) The *Pharisees* made a sharp distinction between members of the movement and other Jews. Anyone who did not fulfil the Pharisaic requirements for holiness was discriminated against, as being the '*am ha-aretz*, the people of the land. This term was originally used to describe Gentiles living in Palestine (Neh. 10.28). Its transference to Jews shows that they were regarded as aliens. Severe restrictions were placed on commerce with them:

> Anyone who undertakes to be a *haber* (i.e. a member of a Pharisaic fellowship) must not sell either fresh fruit or dried fruit to him; he must not buy fresh fruit from him, he must not stay with him as a guest nor must he accept him in his garb as a guest (Demai 2.3).

Such separatist tendencies were already to be found in the first century AD. In the Gospel of John the Pharisees curse the people 'who do not know the law' (John 7.49). According to the synoptic gospels the Pharisees urged separation from sinners – especially during shared meals (Mark 2.16; Luke 7.39).

(*b*) For the *resistance fighters*, the primary indication of membership of the true Israel was not so much observance of the laws of purity as people's attitude towards the Romans: those who collaborated with them were no longer regarded as members of the people. This is clear in Josephus' retrospective account:

> In those days (viz. of the census) the *sicarii* got together against those who were willing to submit to the Romans and treated them in all respects as enemies, plundering them of their possessions, driving

away their cattle and setting fire to their houses. For they said that there was no difference between them and foreigners (*BJ* 7.8.1, §§254f.).

Here part of a domestic group is alienated.

(*c*) For the *Essenes*, membership of the true Israel was not dependent on human activity: it was derived from the unfathomable election of God's will (cf. *Antt.* 13.5.9, §172). God had chosen two spirits, the spirit of light and the spirit of darkness (1QS 3.15). Both determined human actions. The spirit of light and truth was to be found only in the Essene community. All the others were lost. The commandment to love, which in the Old Testament related to all members of the people and even to the strangers in the land (Lev. 19.18,34), was expressly limited to the Essene community. It was the duty of each of its members 'to love all the sons of light, each according to his part in the counsel of God, and hate all the sons of darkness each according to his guilt in the vengeance of God' (1QS 1.9ff.).

(*d*) In the *Jesus movement*, intra-cultural demarcations predominated over inter-cultural ones. This principle is expressed in the Sermon on the Mount: 'Unless your righteousness exceeds that of the scribes and Pharisees, you will never enter the kingdom of heaven' (Matt. 5.20). In this way the Pharisees are denied membership of the true Israel, which is reserved for those who wait upon the kingdom of God (Matt. 21.43). It is consistent for exclusion from the community to be identified with exclusion from the people. Matthew 18.17 states that someone excluded from the community 'is to be to you as a Gentile and a tax collector'. True, the command to love one's enemy transcends all boundaries within groups and outside them. However, precisely by means of this commandment it is possible to study how difficult it is in fact to transcend these boundaries. For love of one's enemy is a sign of being superior to Gentiles and tax-collectors, who know only a love based on mutual advantage (Matt. 5.46f.). Here, too, it is impossible to fulfil the commandment without withdrawing from an outside group.

Thus the attempt to preserve the cultural identity of Judaism by intensifying the norms of the law leads to schism. In extreme cases, members of the various renewal movements persecuted one another. Among the Pharisees, bloody controversies seem to have arisen between the followers of Hillel and those of Shammai. The Pharisee Paul persecuted the Jesus movement (Gal. 1.23; Phil. 3.6). Violent action against others was obviously part of the pro- gramme of the resistance movement. From conflicts of this kind we can judge how far schisms had developed within Judaism. The Jews were involved in a deep crisis of identity, and only the catastrophe of AD 70 gave them the chance to overcome this crisis on the basis of Pharisaism.

4. Causes

Our hypothesis is that the tendencies to intensify norms within Jewish renewal movements are a reaction to the drift towards assimilation produced by superior alien cultures. The first evidence for this connection was produced by the observation that tendencies to intensify norms are often caused by concern for inter-cultural segregation. Further evidence was given by the fact that the most important renewal movements (the Essenes, the Pharisees, the resistance fighters) arose out of the confrontation with alien cultures: the Hasidim of the second century BC, the forerunners of Essenes and Pharisees, opposed the Hellenistic reform programme of those who, with Syrian support, were intent on making Jerusalem into a city state, with the aim of integrating Judaism into Hellenistic culture. The resistance movement of the first century AD was a reaction to the growing influence of the Romans and the renewed upsurge of Hellenistic culture which came with it. Thus socio-cultural tensions between Judaism and Hellenism would be recognizable sociological causes for tendencies to intensify norms in Judaism. These tensions are interpreted in too one-sided a way if we see in them the conflict between an ethnocentric and a cosmopolitan culture. Rather, here we have an encounter of two cultures with world-wide claims, one of which reacts to the claims of the other with ethnocentric attitudes, whether of antisemitism or xenophobia.

(i) *Universalist tendencies in Hellenism and Judaism*[30]
 (a) *Hellenism*. The Hellenistic kingdoms, with their inter-

national populations, were the social basis for the idea that all
men are the citizens of one world state. The idea of cosmopolitanism was formulated for the first time in the territories newly won
over by Hellenism (cf. Zeno, *SVF* 1, 262). At the same time,
however, elements of Greek ethnocentricism were preserved.
Distaste for alien barbarians was now transferred to the
uneducated. Only the wise man was a citizen of the world state.
Ideas of this kind also flourished in Palestine. Meleager of Gadara
composed the epigram:

> Tyre gave me birth, but Gadara was my home, that new Athens in the
> land of the Assyrians . . . If I was a Syrian, what matter? The world is
> the home of mortals, and a chaos bore all men, my friend (*Anthologia
> Graeca* 7.417.1ff.).

This epigram mentions two roots of Hellenistic cosmopolitanism:
common education (cf. the key-word 'Athens') and the common
mythology that goes with it (cf. the key-word 'chaos').

There must have been a flourishing and well-developed system
of education in the city states of Palestine and Syria, since they
produced a wealth of philosophers of very varied allegiances, even
if for the most part they were active outside their homeland.[31]
Mention should be made of the Cynics Menippus, Meleager and
Oenomaus from Gadara; the Sceptic Heraclitus from Tyre; the
Epicureans Zeno from Sidon and Philodemus from Gadara; the
Peripatetics Diodore from Tyre, Boethus from Sidon and
Nicolaus from Damascus; the Stoics Posidonius from Apamea,
Antiochus from Ashkelon, who in the first century BC was direc-
tor of the Academy in Athens, Antipater from Tyre, the teacher
of Cato the younger, and so on. The flourishing intellectual life of
the province also extended to Jewish Palestine. In the Hellenistic
reform attempt in the second century BC, progressive citizens
attempted to set up a gymnasium even in Jerusalem (II
Macc.4.9). The reaction of the Maccabees put an end to that.
However, the fascination remained. It led to attempts by
Josephus and Philo to present the Jewish renewal movements as
philosophical schools, for example the Pharisees as Stoics (*Vita* 2,
§12), the Essenes as Pythagoreans (*Antt.* 15.10.4, §371) or as
ethicists (*Every Good Man* 12, §80).

The universalistic character of Hellenism was also evident in its religion. Greek mythology was transplanted to Syria and Palestine, or native traditions were given a Greek interpretation. Thus the story was told in Joppa of how Perseus freed Andromeda on a rock there (Pliny, *Hist.nat.* V. 13.69; Josephus, *BJ* 3.9.3, §420). Scythopolis prided itself on being the place where Dionysus was brought up (Pliny, *Hist.nat.* V.18.74). In Samaria, in the first century AD, Simon Magus could give out that his consort was a reincarnation of Helen (Justin, *Dial.* 120.6; *Apol.* 26.3). In the same region, Heracles and Astarte were later held to be the parents of Melchizedek in the Old Testament (Epiphanius, *Adv.haer.* 55.2). Apollo was worshipped in Gaza (*Antt.* 1.13.3, §364) and Astarte in Ashkelon as the heavenly Aphrodite (Pausanias I 14.7). During the Hellenistic reform attempt Yahweh was even worshipped as Zeus in Jerusalem and Samaria (II Macc. 6.2; *Antt.* 12.5.5, §261). Hellenistic culture sensed the same god behind the various divine figures. The Maccabean reaction suppressed such beginnings of religious tolerance and withdrew Judaism from the more universalist tendencies of Hellenism. It also resisted from the very beginning the new universalist 'symbol' of the Roman era, the emperor cult.

(*b*) *Universalist tendencies in Judaism.* The universalist claim of Judaism, like Hellenistic cosmopolitanism, was unrestricted ethnocentricism. The Jews hoped that one day all nations would recognize the only true God and would stream to his temple from all points of the compass (Zech. 14.16; Isa.60.1ff.; Matt.8.11). Rule of the world would then pass over to Israel. This belief in the chosen people is without question ethnocentric belief. But it was modified. Israel was chosen only in so far as it fulfilled the demands of God. The great Old Testament prophets had argued that God could also reject Israel. The Deuteronomistic historians had interpreted the whole of Israelite history as far as the Babylonian exile in the light of the prophetic accusations. Thus Israel not only made a great claim in terms of the world; it also directed this claim critically against itself. This happened at the latest stage in the figure of John the Baptist, who warned the Jews against relying on their status as children of Abraham, seeing that God could raise up children for himself out of stones (Matt. 3.9). Thus there are universalist claims in Judaism as well as in

Hellenism. The only difference was that the course of history appeared to confirm the claims of Hellenistic and Roman culture, and to refute those of Judaism. At all events, the universalist claims of Judaism were confirmed by the diaspora. There were Jews everywhere: 'It is not easy to find a place in the world which does not harbour this people and which is not in their hands' (*Antt.* 14.7.2, §115). The lofty nature of monotheism, spiritual worship without sacrifice (in the diaspora), the ethical force of the decalogue and the inner solidarity of the synagogues exercised great powers of attraction on outsiders, so that some of them attached themselves to the Jewish community as 'God-fearers' (cf. Acts 13.34; 16.4, etc.), or made the decision to have themselves circumcised and to become proselytes (Matt. 23.15; Acts 6.5). On the whole, however, Judaism tended to be on the defensive: its special role as the people destined to rule the world seemed to be threatened.

(ii) *Ethnocentric reactions in Hellenism and in Judaism*   Peoples and nations have a socio-cultural identity when they accept themselves and are accepted by others in various roles. Hellenism and Judaism, however, found it difficult to accept each other. Here two universalist claims were in competition. Moreover, traditional ethnocentricism continued in both these claims. In conflicts, both sides resorted to it. The Romans, whom we may count as representatives of Hellenistic culture, were not prepared to allow their world mission to be opposed in principle by a small people. Tacitus speaks of the 'bitterness that the Jews alone had not conformed' (*Hist.* V.10). In turn, the Jews maintained their eschatological claim to power and expected that one day in the future they would rule the world.

(a) In antiquity there was *antisemitism* at all levels of society,[32] even with such educated men as Poseidonius, Cicero, Seneca and Tacitus. The upper classes feared the Jewish minority as a potential *élite*. Seneca expresses this relatively clearly when he says of the Jews: 'The customs of that most criminal nation have become so strong that they are now spread over all lands: the vanquished have given laws to the vanquishers' (Augustine, *Civitas Dei* VI.11). Three conditions of ancient antisemitism are worth stressing:

(1) An ambivalent attitude towards Judaism, hesitation between recognition and repudiation. The monotheism, the ethical standards and the solidarity of Jewish communities were very attractive. Antisemitic prejudice had the function, among others, of working against them. What was seen in a positive light by the majority had inevitably to be presented as a 'notorious vice' when observed in the context of a minority which was discriminated against (Philo, *Leg. ad Gaium* 18–20, §§120–33). Leisure was highly prized in antiquity, but for the Jewish people to celebrate every seventh day as a rest day was taken as a sign of sloth. Help among friends was much treasured in antiquity, but solidarity among Jews was regarded as suspicious (Cicero, *Pro Flacco* 82.66). This hesitation between recognition and repudiation is expressed in Strabo's theory of decadence (16.2.35ff.). In it, Moses is celebrated as a wise and godfearing man, but his successors are censured for making food laws and circumcision obligatory.

(2) Prejudices were also encouraged by the combination of the minority status of the diaspora Jews and their solidarity which extended beyond any particular region. There was a Jewish lobby everywhere. This sort of situation favoured suspicions of conspiracies. Even Cicero made use of this clumsy means of defending his client Flaccus against the charges of the Jews. With an eye to the numerous Jews involved in the trial he pointed out 'what a great crowd they are, how they keep together and how influential they are in assemblies' (*Pro Flacco* 82.66).

(3) Within the Roman empire the Jews were both discriminated against and afforded special privileges, and this also led to prejudice against them. They had been able to keep more of their independence than other peoples. They were exempt from the cult of the emperor. They were seldom conscripted for military service. This could cause resentment. The 'Acts of the Pagan Martyrs' which come from Alexandria complain about the privileges accorded to the Jews by the Romans and combine anti-Roman and antisemitic tendencies. Aggression against the Romans was transformed into aggression against a minority who could be identified with the Romans on the grounds of their privileges, but the Romans did not identify themselves with the Jews in any degree that might have made them feel that an attack

on the Jews was an attack on them. Even in antiquity, the Jews were an ideal scapegoat.

(*b*) *Xenophobia in Judaism*. Judaism, too, ultimately based its way of encountering alien cultures on ethnocentric attitudes. In this it was no different from other peoples. Certainly it made severe demands on itself. But precisely these self-critical demands could further ethnocentric reactions. The identity of Israel was grounded in the law; the more seriously it took the law, the greater had to be its concern over its own failure and the loss of identity which followed from that. This concern was projected on to objects and people which were regarded as 'unclean'. It turned into anxiety about defilement which was conceived of in naturalistic terms, anxiety about coming into contact with anything alien or Gentile:

> If anyone buys any cooking utensils from a Gentile, he must immerse whatever is usually purified by immersion; he must scald out whatever is usually purified by scalding, and he must sterilize with fire whatever is usually sterilized with fire (Abodah Zarah 5.12).

Anxiety about infection from Gentiles governed even the most basic human relationships. Jews only married among themselves. Food regulations made social contact with Gentiles difficult; they ate at separate tables (*separati epulis*, Tacitus, *Hist.* V.5). They lived in their own districts (e.g. in Alexandria), 'the better to be able to preserve the purity of their way of life, uncontaminated with aliens' (*BJ* 2.18.7, §488). All these phobias about contact can be interpreted as anxiety over a loss of self-identity in Judaism projected on to people and things. The baptist movement which emerged at the end of the first century BC is incomprehensible apart from this anxiety. John the Baptist appealed to anxiety over a loss of self-identity when he questioned whether being a child of Abraham was a guarantee of salvation (Matt. 3.9). Jesus, too, came from this baptist movement. However, among his followers anxiety over loss of identity gave way to a new certainty, to trust in the grace of God.

5. Summary

If a people ascribes to itself a privileged role among all the nations but is threatened with eclipse by the political or cultural

superiority of other groups, it will inevitably be involved in a
serious crisis of identity. Its image of itself is threatened and its
inner equilibrium is destroyed. Israel went through such a crisis
of identity in the first century AD. It was necessary for unfavour-
able historical experiences to be incorporated laboriously into the
Jews' image of themselves. Dependence on foreigners could be
interpreted as a punishment for offences committed by the
people, while the deeper ethical sensitivity which it produced could
in turn strengthen awareness of the difference between the Jews
and other peoples. The more problematical Jewish socio-cultural
identity became in the present, the more intensive the expectation
that this identity would be achieved in reality in the future.
Intensification of norms and accentuation of eschatological expectations seemed to be the way out of the crisis of Jewish self-
identity. But in the end they led to an even more profound crisis.
For the intensification of norms inevitably produced schism among
the Jews, with several renewal movements in competition with
one another. In that situation, agreement about who was the 'true
Israel' was possible only within a particular group. All the others
ceased to be regarded as true Jews. Once the stage had been
reached when birth and descent were no longer acceptable as the
criteria for membership of true Judaism, the next step was not far
away. In principle, why should not anyone participate in the
privileged role of the true Israel? Just as inter-cultural segregation
inevitably led to schisms within a culture, so this development of
schisms led to the universalization of Judaism. This universalization inevitably broke through when the intensification of norms
became the relaxation of norms, and when it was recognized that
even an elect remnant within Israel could not satisfy these intensified norms: all, Jews and Gentiles alike, were directed towards
grace. The break-through happened in the Jesus movement,
though it was only with Paul that its final consequences were
drawn. Traditional ethnocentricism was not, however, finally
superseded, but transformed into a new factor: the claim of the
church to absoluteness was a metamorphosis of ethnocentricism.
Now it was the church which understood itself as the chosen
people and all outsiders were treated as Gentiles. An ethnocen-
trically tinged conception of all foreigners was taken over from

Judaism. It would have been better if the church had also taken over from Judaism rather more of that inexorable self-critism which distinguishes Jewish ethnocentricism from all others.

This brings our analysis of factors to an end. If we make a distinction between theories of integration and theories of conflict in the sociology of religion it should be noted that the latter clearly fit better into an analysis of the Jesus movement. Where-ever we look we find deep-rooted tensions, tensions between productive groups and those who enjoy the profit, between city and country, between alien and native structures of government, between Hellenistic and Jewish culture. This is the situation from which the Jesus movement emerged, and it was partly conditioned by these tensions, while at the same time having its own effect on them. The crisis in Palestinian-Jewish society had led to the search for new patterns of religious and social life. It had put in question traditional values and modes of behaviour. Social life was threatened with anomie, which results when numerous members of a society are no longer able to live their lives in accordance with the norms of their traditional environment because the groups to which they belong have changed in status and as a result their traditional norms and values have been shattered. Anomie is not restricted to particular classes in society. At a time of increasing social tensions it affects all classes, upper and lower class alike, those whose expectations are rising and those who are on the decline. (All that can be said is that marginal groups are probably most sensitive to situations of this kind and that it is among them that a longing for social and religious renewal often arises.) One instance is the rise of Islam. The conflict between Byzantium and Persia had diverted trade to Arabia in the seventh century AD, Mecca was enjoying an economic boom and the new prosperity had put traditional values in question: 'In short, this was a situation of anomie, and it resulted in the formation of a new religious movement led by a native of Mecca named Muhammad.'[33] The rise of Islam illustrates the fact that crises of social and religious orientation could also be brought about by new prosperity. Thus the interpretation of early Palestinian Christianity presented here in terms of crisis should not be taken to suggest that the Jesus movement simply arose out of social need, economic pressure and political repression. Rich men were also among its members. However, members of the middle classes whose status was threatened are likely to have predominated. In any event, many factors contributed to that crisis of orientation in society to which the Jesus movement sought to give an answer. To the extent to which this answer can be analysed in sociological terms, it is the object of functional analysis by sociologists of religion.

Part Three

Analysis of Function: The Effects of the Jesus Movement on Society

The analysis of factors has shown that the Jesus movement emerged out of a deep-seated crisis in Palestinian Jewish society. If it were no more than a reflection of social conditions, an analysis of its social conditioning would be conclusive; a separate analysis of function would be unnecessary. However, we proceed on the assumption that the Jesus movement not only emerged from a social crisis but also articulated an answer to this crisis which does not have a sociological derivation. This assumption is not made on arbitrary grounds: the following considerations will help to justify it.

(*a*) The social crisis explains why renewal movements came into being. It does not explain the particular form of the renewal movements. We can explain why there was widespread social rootlessness in Palestine at that tine, but not why one man became a criminal, another a holy man, the third an emigrant and the fourth an ascetic. Sociological explanations only apply to typical features and not to individual instances. They simply mark out a certain area and cannot account for what happens within this area. Thus religious phenomena have a 'relative autonomy'. Social factors leave room for varied conduct.

(*b*) A sociological analysis may be able to illuminate the genesis of religious phenomena, but it does not explain their effect or lack of effect. Something that comes into being for social reasons can be handed on for its own sake. Thus social rootlessness originally had primarily economic grounds. Once it had become widespread, however, the pattern of behaviour associated with it could also be imitated for quite different reasons. Consequently in many cases we shall have to accord socially conditioned religious phenomena a 'functional autonomy': their effect cannot be derived from their origin.

(*c*) Finally, an analysis of religious phenomena cannot ignore religious self-understanding and its awareness of its own autonomy. Even a theoretical approach which would completely deny the independence of religion could continue to interpret its claim to autonomy as a significant human action, as a protest against the heteronomous complex of conditioning factors over which it stands. Thus religion would possess 'oppositional autonomy'.[34]

If religious phenomena have at least relative, functional and oppositional autonomy, an analysis of the effects of religious phenomena cannot be identical with an analysis of the factors which condition them, since as a result of these religious phenomena new elements come into play which cannot be derived from the conditioning factors. Now an analysis of function does not investigate all effects, but only those which have some reference to the objective, basic aims of society. When a society is involved in a crisis, its chief concern is to overcome and reduce the tensions within itself. It has to consider questions like: should the tensions be increased to the point of rebellion? Is it necessary to provide opportunities for letting off steam? Is there a need for compromise? Faced with a crisis, every society attempts different solutions. The experiments are usually carried out among small groups of outsiders. Society as a whole approves particular elements from their functional outlines (which are not identical with the stated aims of particular groups, since they also include unintentional consequences), changes them or develops them further. Nevertheless, the results of this activity usually remain unused and atrophied on the fringes of society. There is a good deal of unnecessary social experimentation; this is again a matter of function, since the needs of society are not known to begin with. Jewish society in Palestine also experimented in this way. By various means the renewal movements which emerged within Judaism sought to overcome increasing tensions. Only a little of their activity has made a lasting mark, but among what remains is the work of the Jesus movement: they experimented with a vision of love and reconciliation.

IX. The Functional Outline of the Jesus Movement

Tensions give rise to forms of aggression. The overcoming of tension therefore always means the overcoming of aggression. In my view, the best description of the functional outline of the Jesus movement for overcoming social tensions is an interpretation of it as a contribution towards containing and overcoming aggression. In this connection, four forms of containing aggression emerge: aggression was: (1) compensated for by counter-impulses; (2) transferred to other objects and ascribed to other subjects; (3) internalized and reversed so as to fall on the subject of the aggression; (4) depicted in christological symbols and transformed. In each instances two separate problems may be noted: the problem of the subject's aggression, which is expressed actively, and the problem of the aggression which derives from others.[35]

1. Compensation for aggression

The tendency towards aggression is countered in the Jesus movement with the commandment to love, and the aggression which is made more radical by social tensions is countered by a more radical version of this commandment: 'You have heard that it was said, "You shall love your neighbour and hate your enemy." But I say to you, Love your enemies and pray for those who persecute you' (Matt. 5.43f.). In fact, members of 'enemy' groups, a tax-collector (Mark 2.14) and a zealot (Luke 6.15), belonged to the circle of the disciples. Groups which were discriminated against were accepted by the Jesus movement. The radical form of the love commandment could be interpreted in psycho-analytical terms as a pattern of reaction: intensified aggressiveness turns into its opposite. Drives which originally served aggressive ends now work in the opposite direction. This becomes even clearer in connection with the problem of aggression shown by outsiders. Here the compensation for aggression amounts to forgiveness and reconciliation. This is required, not seven times, but seventy-seven times (Matt. 18.21f.). Here reference is made to Gen. 4.24, where there is a boast of sevenfold vengeance for Cain, but of seventy-sevenfold vengeance for Lamech. It is clear that the energy which had previously been devoted to impulses towards vengeance was now to serve contrary impulses. So we may in no wise conclude from the eirenic character of the Jesus movement that it was made up of a group of people with diminished aggressive impulses. On the contrary, the intensity of the compensation points to the intensity of the repressed inclinations. What by everyday standards is irrational love of enemies is indirect evidence of the strength of the aggressive impulses which have to be overcome. Since we cannot simply assume that these impulses disappeared, we must also look for them in their new manifestation.

2. The transference of aggression

Aggression which cannot be compensated for by impulses in the opposite direction keeps appearing as an impulse which is either ascribed to a vicarious subject (the object in this case can remain the same) or is directed against a vicarious object (in which case the subject can remain the same). In particular, supernatural figures (God, the Son of man, demons) take the place of human partners. Whether actively or passively, they take over existing aggression and thus relieve ordinary human relationships of it. When we take into account the distinction between the subject's aggression and the aggression which derives from others, we have four possible ways of transferring aggression:

	Subject's aggression	Aggression from others
Substitution of subject	Vicarious subject: the Son of man as eschatological judge	Vicarious subject: God as the omnipotent one
Substitution of object	Shift to a vicarious object: aggression against the demons	Shift to a vicarious victim: the humiliated Son of man

(*a*) *Substitution of the subject of aggression.* Anyone who has suffered an injury without reacting aggressively often punishes the aggressor in his imagination by visualizing how he experiences suffering at the hands of a third party. This also happened in the Jesus movement. If the early Christian wandering charismatics were rejected in a place, they visualized the eschatological judgment being realized upon it: 'It shall be more tolerable on the day of judgment for the land of Sodom and Gomorrah than for that town' (Matt. 10.15). They were convinced that the Son of man would not forgive sins against the holy Spirit – i.e. against the prophetic spirit which spoke through them (Matt. 12.31f.). By identifying themselves with the Son of man they could project their aggression into an eschatological future and delegate the performance of aggressive actions to the Son of man: 'Whoever is ashamed of me and of my words in this adulterous and sinful generation, of him will the Son of man also be ashamed, when he comes . . .' (Mark 8.38). And if their own aggression could be delegated, the aggression of others could be ascribed to another subject. In the last resort, everything is in God's hands. He has counted the hairs on a man's head. Why then fear those who kill the body? (Luke 12.4–7).

(*b*) *Substitution of the object of aggression.* In psychoanalysis, the shift of a drive to another goal which is not in fact directly connected with the original goal is known as 'transference'. We also find this way of dealing with aggression in the Jesus movement. Aggression against the Romans seems to have been transferred to demons, as is shown by the exorcism on the coasts of Gadara (Mark 5.1ff.). The demons who live in the herd of swine behave like an occupying power. They speak Latin, present themselves as 'legion', and like the Romans have only one wish:

to be allowed to stay in the country. The way in which they are
drowned in the lake along with the swine corresponds to the
hostile thoughts directed against the Romans by the Jewish
people: they would dearly like to see the Romans driven into the
sea. The connection between foreign rule and the rule of demons
is a plausible one: foreign gods and foreign forms of worship
came into the country with the Romans. Even the Roman stan-
dard was under suspicion as an idol, which is why its presence in
the holy city of Jerusalem led to protests (1QpHab 6.3ff.; *Antt.*
18.3.1, §§55ff.; 18.5.3, §121). And idols were regarded as demons
(Deut. 33.17; Ps. 95.5; Eth.Enoch 19.1; 99.7; Jub. 1.11; I Cor.
10.20). The longer Roman rule lasted, the greater must have been
the impression that demons had taken over the rule of Israel from
God, especially as this view found new life in traditional patterns
of interpretation. Alien Syrian rule had been interpreted in a
similar way. In the apocalypse of the shepherds (Eth. Enoch 85–
90), which was composed at that time, on the loss of Israel's
political independence God delegated his rule to seventy shepherds who wilfully tormented the people (85.59ff.). They were
to be condemned at the end of days (90.22ff.). These shepherds
were demons, i.e. fallen angels and subjects of Satan. Among the
Essenes, the war against the nations at the end of days was also
seen as a war against Belial and his hosts (1QM 1.9ff.). We may
conclude from this that if anyone sees a fight against his political
opponents as a fight against Satan, then a fight against Satan and
his subjects will also be a fight against political opponents. So
when Jesus says, 'If it is by the finger of God that I cast out
demons, then the kingdom of God has come upon you' (Luke
11.20), his saying is not entirely unpolitical.[36] Exorcisms were
acts of liberation transposed into the mythical sphere. The
demons functioned as vicarious objects of the aggression of the
Jesus movement. But there was also a 'substitute' for the aggression they experienced from others. Whatever was endured by
members of the Jesus movement was in the end also endured by
the Son of man. In the person of the least of his brothers he was
despised, put to shame and persecuted (Matt. 25.40).

3. The reversal of aggression

One of the most remarkable forms of coping with aggression in the Jesus movement is the reversal of aggression against the aggressor – not as an aggressive action but as a moral reproach and an unspoken appeal to give up aggression. In so far as the concern is to overcome the aggression of members of the movement, here aggression is internalized and introjected. We can see introjected aggressiveness in the call to repentance and the imperatives based on intensification of norms. Luke 13.1ff. is a significant instance of this. Pilate had massacred Galilean pilgrims. Feelings against him ran high. But Jesus says, 'Do you think that these Galileans were worse sinners than all the other Galileans, because they suffered this? I tell you, No; but unless you repent you will all likewise perish' (13.2f.). Here rebelliousness against the Romans is diverted elsewhere: it is not a matter of Roman guilt, but of one's own guilt. Rebellion against the Romans becomes rebellion against oneself. It is interesting that we find other instances than the power structures of the Roman empire in connection with the demand for repentance. Foreign city states (Matt. 11.20ff.) and a foreign queen (Matt. 12.42) are cited to give emphasis to the demand for repentance. Comparison with foreigners amounts to an appeal to the Israelite understanding that its privileged special role among the nations brings obligations with it. Anxiety over the loss of this special role is already a motive for the call to repentance in the preaching of John the Baptist (Matt. 3.7ff.).

Now a call to repentance and the intensification of norms were widespread in the Judaism of the time. Among all movements, some degree of aggression against foreigners was transformed into self-criticism. What was the special characteristic of the followers of John the Baptist and Jesus here? We saw that tendencies to intensify norms, which were intended to preserve the national characteristics from being assimilated into the surrounding environment, in fact led to schisms. To put it another way: the heightened aggressiveness introduced by the reaction of intensified norms at the same time led to heightened aggressiveness against anyone who did not observe the accentuated norms. The people was fragmented into groups, each of which repudiated the other. These tendencies towards particularization provoked a counter-movement. Once the norms had been intensified still further, so that they were quite beyond the possibility of fulfilment, all alike, whether pious or impious, radical or moderate, faced the threat of divine judgment. In that case no group could continue to claim that it alone was the 'true Israel'. Nor could anyone claim to offer anything better. All alike were sinners.

Thus the introduction of heightened aggressiveness could lead, paradoxically, to a positive acceptance of the other. This change was ushered in with the preaching of John the Baptist. It confronted all men with God's imminent wrath: 'You brood of vipers! Who warned you to flee from the wrath to come?' (Matt. 3.7). The question was rhetorical. For John the Baptist, it was a certainty that no one could escape the wrath of God unless he was baptized as a sign of his repentance. The Jesus movement developed out of the baptist movement, but differed from it in three characteristic points:

(*a*) John the Baptist lived in the wilderness. He based his withdrawal there on the very quotation from the Bible which the Qumran community used to justify their existence in the wilderness (Mark 1.3; 1QS 8.14; 9.19f.). His retreat from society was symptomatic. People had to leave unhealthy society behind if they were to come to the Baptist. The Jesus movement was different: its members wandered over the settled areas of the country and sought people out in their homes.

(*b*) This geographical separation matched the ascetic features of the baptist movement. John neither ate nor drank – unlike Jesus (Matt. 11.18f.). The Jesus movement, too, must at one stage have rejected fasting on the grounds: 'Can the wedding guests fast while the bridegroom is with them?' (Mark 2.19a). Here confidence in a time of joy takes the place of eschatological anxiety.

(*c*) The decisive difference lay in the different understandings of judgment and grace. For John the Baptist's movement, repentance and baptism were the only way of being saved from judgment. It cannot be a coincidence that Jesus did not practise baptism. If the urge to be baptized is based on eschatological anxiety, then a decline in this anxiety must be matched by a retreat from baptism. Furthermore, the demand for repentance can now be motivated by the joy of God who delights more in one penitent sinner than in ninety-nine just men (Luke 15.7). It is grounded in the dawning of the kingdom of God (Mark 1.15). And this kingdom of God is presented as a compelling mystery, as a wedding feast, treasure in a field, a pearl. The great mystery of judgment to some extent retreats into the background. This is also clear from minor details. In Matt. 12.38ff., Jonah and Solomon are used as types to illustrate Jesus' call to repentance. The former is a prophet whose announcement of judgment is thwarted by God's grace; the latter a king who fascinated a foreign queen with his wisdom. Neither of them were gloomy preachers of repentance.

The decisive shift from John the Baptist to the Jesus movement consisted in the way in which the radical intensification of the demands of the Torah was grounded in and limited by a radical proclamation of the grace of God. Introjected aggressiveness turned into self-acceptance on the basis of the divine love. The most important precondition for this was the anxiety-free atmosphere which emerges so clearly from the parables. It is as though primal confidence in life had been given a new and powerful impulse. If we remember the connection between anxiety and aggression we can understand why the overcoming of aggression in the Jesus movement could become a particular vision of society.

In the last resort, we cannot give any reasons for the transformation of ethical radicalism into a radical proclamation of the grace of God. We can, however, observe it at many points in the synoptic tradition. In connection with the story of the rich young man, the question is raised: 'If no rich man can enter the kingdom of God, then who can be saved?' The answer is: 'With men it is impossible, but not with God, for all things are possible with God' (Mark 10.27). The impossibility of fulfilling the intensified norms here becomes a pointer towards the grace of God. This is also the case with some of the intensified demands in the antitheses in the Sermon on the Mount. Certainly, they are meant to be realized. But subtle distinctions are nevertheless made. On two occasions stress is laid only on the contradiction between conduct and the norm: 'Every one who is angry with his brother shall be liable to judgment' (Matt. 5.22). 'Every one who looks at a woman lustfully has already committed adultery with her in his heart' (Matt. 5.28). There is significance in the formulations which have been chosen. The intensification of the commandments against killing and against adultery makes impossible demands on every man: aggressive dispositions and erotic fascination cannot be made subject to human wills. Anyone who requires that is asking for the impossible. Even the Jesus movement seems to have suspected this. For within the Sermon on the Mount as it is now presented in Matthew there follow further admonitions which presuppose what has already been prohibited *de facto*: Matt. 5.23 requires reconciliation in view of discord which already exists, while Matt. 5.29 mentions self-mutilation in the case of offences, thereby presupposing the corresponding dispositions. Thus it is significant that in each case the prohibitions are not formulated as instructions for action. The statements are not put in the imperative: 'You shall not sin', 'You shall not have sexual feelings towards another woman.' What we have instead is a statement in the indicative that the angry man is no better than the murderer, the lustful man no better than the adulterer. Such an approach to the question of guilt makes self-righteous assessments of transgressions of norms impossible. It compels the recognition that there is no crime for which we do not have the inner drive. In contrast to the two antitheses which we considered above, the prohibition against oaths is formulated as an instruction for action. There were in fact no physical obstacles in the way of refusing to give an oath. This practice was to be found a number of groups in Judaism. Elsewhere, however, many of the intensified norms (also) culminate in the recognition that all men ultimately fail, that they are all directed towards the grace of God, that it is senseless to condemn others without perceiving the plank in one's own eye (Matt. 7.3ff.). It is senseless to seek separation from sinners if no one is good but God (Mark 10.18). It is absurd to cast the first stone (John 8.1ff.). Self-righteousness is a sin even if one is unaware of any sin: that is why the publican goes to his house justified, unlike the self-righteous Pharisee (Luke 18.10ff.). In the New Testament, we find for the first time the revolutionary – and healthy – insight that to take any human ethical requirement seriously will demonstrate its inadequacy, that ethics without forgiveness is a perversion, and that there is more to morality than morality, if it is to remain human. This recognition certainly points far beyond the particular historical context in which it came into being. But at one time it was a contribution towards overcoming a deep-rooted crisis in Judaism. The identity of Judaism could not be achieved by rival intensifications of the demands of the Torah, each of which sought to outbid the others; the only answer was the recognition of divine grace. In the last resort, solidarity between men could not be achieved by an intensification of norms; this could only heighten latent and open aggressiveness. What was needed was a new relationship to all norms: putting trust and freedom from anxiety before demands of any kind.

This way of dealing with the group's own introjected aggression is matched by its reflection of the aggression directed towards it back on the aggressors. The Old Testament 'an eye for an eye and a tooth for a tooth' is no longer to apply. Rather, the commandment is: 'Do not resist one who is evil. But if anyone strikes you on the right cheek, turn to him the other also' (Matt. 5.39). The purpose of this demonstration of a rejection of self-defence is to cause aggressors to reflect. It is as though the Jesus movement here postulates a human inhibition against aggression which does not yet exist, of the kind that we can observe in animals when the victim indicates his surrender by a provocative attitude of defencelessness. In the animal realm this inhibition against aggression is instinctual; among men, however, it calls for deliberate self-control and is an ethical task. Mahatma Gandhi and Martin Luther King have given it new and impressive form in our own time. They too hoped for the paradoxical transformation of power into powerlessness, of aggression into reconciliation, by appealing to the standards of their opponents in rejecting the possibility of self-defence. Of course this appeal comprises a sublimated form of aggression, namely a reproach based on the fact that the other will accept it of his own free will – without compulsion. The hope is that part of his aggression will be directed inwards, so that new aggressive actions call forth shame and an awareness of guilt. We also find this method of dealing with aggression in the symbols of christology. The execution of Jesus was a repressive measure carried out by the Romans. But it did not call forth any rebelliousness against the Romans within the Jesus movement. They accepted defeat. The cross became the sign of salvation. It was a revelation, not of Roman guilt but of their own: Jesus had to die for our sins. The failed Messiah became the bringer of salvation. We can see the significance of this development from a comparison with other failed messianic figures. Thus Antigonus, the last Hasmonaean king, was executed by the Romans, having first been bound to a stake and scourged (Dio Cassius 49.22.6). The intention was to make it impossible for the Jews to identify themselves with his fate:

> He [i.e. Antony] was the first of the Romans to have a king killed with the axe; for he thought that this was the only way in which the Jews could be brought to recognize Herod as king in his place . . ., so high was the opinion which they had of their kings. So he believed that by this shameful death memory of him would be wiped out among the Jews and their hatred towards Herod would be diminished (Strabo, according to *Antt.* 15.1.2, §9).

Antony had little success. After Herod's death, messianic pretenders arose everywhere. They too failed. Simon was beheaded; Athronges seems to have fallen into the hands of Archelaus. In addition, many of the followers of these messiahs were crucified: Varus had them nailed to crosses (*Antt.* 17.10.5–8, §§271–94). The Jesus movement was, however, the first to incorporate the failure of a messianic expectation into a religious belief. The execution of the Messiah, which in the case of Antigonus was intended to prevent identification with him, in fact became the occasion for a heightened form of identification: the crucified figure was worshipped as God's emissary. The *de facto* impotence of Judaism in the face of the Romans was accepted in the form of religious symbols and in this way the Roman empire was won: a kerygmatic appeal went forth from the defenceless victims to which in due course even the former victors had to yield.

4. The symbolization of aggression

We have already pointed on several occasions to the significance of christological symbolism for the way in which aggression was dealt with the Jesus movement. Symbolization means more than the representation of psycho-dynamic forces which exist independently of the symbols. Symbolization is a way of guiding and influencing this process. The fluidity of social relationships in Palestinian Jewish society, and the aggressiveness to be found within them, necessitated a reduction of tensions and aggression. There were frequent quests for a scapegoat, for hostile groups inside society or beyond it, which would serve as a means of relaxing the accumulated tensions. The Jesus movement went against this tendency. It ostentatiously accepted the traditional scapegoats: foreigners, tax-collectors, sinners. It pointed to another 'scapegoat', who exceeded all others in his capacity for absorbing aggression: the crucified Jesus was made the scapegoat. At any rate, this is the way in which his death was interpreted from a very early stage (Mark 10.45; 14.24; I Cor. 15.3). The remarkable thing is that when a group chooses someone as a scapegoat, it puts out of mind the fact that in reality he is the victim of its own tensions. It attributes to him a quality which he in fact acquires only in a social setting, as though it were almost native to him. This naivety is lacking in the christological symbolism of the scapegoat. The Son of man deliberately accepted the role of the sacrifice for many (Mark 10.45). What is elsewhere an unconscious development was here made manifest in christological imagery.

It is also worth noting that the aggression transferred to the scapegoat has a double origin. First, he takes over the aggressions of the group, their transgressions of the norm; at the same time, however, he also takes over the aggressiveness of the norm, the law and human conscience: the curse of the law, as Paul puts it (Gal. 3.13). To put it in psycho-analytical terms: he takes over both the aggressiveness of the drives of the Id and that of the strictness of the super-ego, backed up by the God of the law. A third feature is probably the decisive one. Normally the scapegoat is sent into the wilderness, carrying with him there all the ten-

sions of the community (Lev. 16.10). No one bothers about him
any more. Simply to send him away unburdens the community.
But the Jesus movement continued to identify itself with its
'scapegoat'. It ascribed to him the power to triumph over his
expiatory death. It made him the ruler. Here that form of dealing
with life which gains power to rise above suffering, tensions and
guilt by the internalization of negative experiences, found its
compelling symbol:[37] the victim became the priest, the defendant
the judge, the helpless man the ruler of the world, the rejected
one the centre of the community. Without question this is something tremendous, unique. It seems as though for a moment
mankind had managed to overcome the scapegoat complex which
poisons all human relationships. Social relationships would
inevitably look quite different if these symbols were internalized,
and influenced our conduct.

To sum up: a small group of outsiders experimented with a
vision of love and reconciliation in a society which had been put
out of joint, suffering from an excess of tensions, pressures and
forms of aggression, in order to renew this society from within.
The men involved were not lacking in aggressiveness themselves,
nor were they untouched by the tensions of their time. There is
much to suggest the opposite. A good deal of aggression could be
transformed into criticism of riches and possessions, Pharisees
and priests, temple and tabus, and thus be made to serve the new
vision. A good deal of aggression was diverted, transferred,
projected, transformed and symbolized. It was this way of dealing
with aggression that made room for the new vision of love and
reconciliation at whose centre stood the new commandment to
love one's enemy. The origin of the 'vision' itself remains a
riddle. For we can also draw the opposite conclusion: the presupposition for the various ways of dealing with aggression was a
basic attitude which was free of anxiety, a renewed fundamental
trust in the reality which issues from the figure of Jesus – even
down to our own time.

x. Functional Effects

Did the vision of love and reconciliation ever have a chance of being realized? Could it offer a constructive contribution to life in community? In giving an answer we must break the question down further and consider its chances (1) within the Jesus movement itself, (2) within Palestinian Jewish society as a whole, and (3) within the Hellenistic world.

1. The Jesus movement

Obviously the Jesus movement took its own programme seriously. The question is not so much how it was possible to obligate a group to observe such 'alien' demands as that of loving their enemies. This group was in an exceptional situation and consisted of outsiders. The early Christian wandering charismatics in particular had the freedom to put even an extreme ethical pattern into effect. The problem is, rather: how could the Jesus movement cherish the hope of permeating the whole of society with this pattern? Was that not to expect a miracle? And indeed a miracle is what they hoped for. The Jesus movement believed in miracles, in the realization of what appeared to be impossible. It had experienced miracles. For it is beyond question that Jesus had powers beyond that of a normal man. Furthermore, he had the gift of arousing these capabilities in other men. His followers had performed miracles themselves. All these miracles were regarded as signs of the great eschatological revolution: exorcisms announced the coming of the kingdom of God (Matt. 12.28).

Now if the movement had at its disposal powers which foretold a complete change in the world, might it not also have confidence in ethical extremes? Would not the faith which moves mountains (Mark 11.23) also be capable of changing the human heart? If so many miracles had taken place, would not the miracle of love be possible also? We should not underestimate the encouraging effect of miracles. Matthew 11.2–6 combines both Jesus' paranormal actions and his proclamation of the gospel. The message of reconciliation and love is given added force by the fact that the blind are made to see and the sick are healed.

2. Palestinian Jewish society

As a renewal movement within Judaism, the Jesus movement was a failure. It found so little support that the Jewish historian Josephus could largely ignore it. The primary cause of its failure in Palestine may be the growing tensions in Palestinian Jewish society. The Jesus movement had come into being in a comparatively peaceful period. All that Tacitus can write of the time is that things were quiet under Tiberius (*sub Tiberio quies, Hist.* V.9). The unrest after the death of Herod (6 BC) and the first development of an anti-Roman resistance movement after the deposition of Archelaus (AD 4) lay far back in the past. The situation was certainly not without its tensions. There is sufficient evidence of that. But there were no major conflicts, so that it is perhaps no coincidence that a new movement with a propensity towards peace-making came into being in this particular time. In any case, during the thirties, after the death of Jesus, the tensions became more acute: the controversies in Alexandria (in which Palestinians were also involved) and the turbulent events connected with Gaius Caligula's attempt to introduce his statue into the temple (AD 39–40) may have been symptoms of growing conflicts which were intensified further by the great famine under Claudius (*c.* AD 46–48). Now if a society feels threatened and uncertain, it usually resorts to traditional patterns of behaviour; the most sacred treasures of the nation are ostensibly revered, dissociation from anything alien is intensified and currency is given to fanatical slogans. We may assume that events also developed in this direction in Palestinian Jewish society in the first half of the first century AD. However, this development diminished the chances of the Jesus movement, which encroached on the tabus of society with its criticism of the temple and the law. Its attitude to aliens ran contrary to the tendencies towards segregation that we may assume to have been prevalent. Indeed, it is even probable that the Jesus movement was often forced into the role of a scapegoat: antipathy towards aliens could easily be transferred to those who loosened or even broke through the bonds which held the Jews united against foreigners. Social tensions could be expressed in the suppression of minorities. Thus it is hardly by chance that the persecution under Herod Agrippa (AD 41–44) came after the unrest in Alexandria and Palestine. Nor is it coincidence that at the same time Herod Agrippa made enemies of both the Hellenistic cities and the first Christians (Acts 12.20ff.). Acts explicitly stresses that the persecution was carried out to meet the wishes of the 'Jews'. Must there not have been a need among the people to discover scapegoats? The situation of the Christians must have become even more precarious with the increasing tensions that preceded the Jewish war. The Christians belonged to the peace party. There is nothing to support the assumption that they will have taken part in the rebellion against the Romans. It is more probable that at that time many Christians left the country because the situation was becoming intolerable.

We could, of course, argue as follows: Hillelite Pharisaism, too, seems to have had little chance before the Jewish rebellion. It was too prepared for compromise. Why, then, did it establish itself after the rebellion? Why had Christianity no chance at all when it was a matter of consolidating Judaism anew? At this point we come to a second reason for the failure of the Jesus movement in Palestine: the success of primitive Christianity outside Palestine. This success must have had negative effects on the situation of Christians in the land where the movement originated. The clearer it became that Christianity transcended the boundaries of Judaism and would accept even uncircumcised Gentiles, the less chance it had as a renewal movement within Judaism. For it is impossible to reform any group and at the same time to put its

identity in question. The activity of Christian missionaries among
Gentiles must inevitably have given the impression that other
people were being put on the same footing as the Jews. We can
therefore understand why fraternization between Jews and
Gentiles in the community in Antioch was noted with suspicion
by the Jerusalem community (Gal. 2.11ff.), and why Paul was
felt by the Palestinian churches to be encouraging compromise,
so that his fellow-countrymen planned to murder him (Acts
23.12ff.). In order to understand the failure of the Jesus
movement as a renewal movement within Judaism, we must therefore investigate its success in the Hellenistic world. Such
an investigation would go beyond the limits of this attempt
at a sociology of the Jesus movement. We must therefore
content ourselves with giving a brief survey of further develop-
ments.

3. Hellenistic society

Our analysis of the Jesus movement in Palestine was based on
a sociological theory of conflict: religious renewal movements
develop out of social tensions and attempt to give new impulses
for their resolution. In small groups of outsiders, society experimented with new forms of life, but chose only a few elements
from the wealth of new possibilities which emerged, adapting
them to its needs. Much remained unused. A negative selection
was made even from the Jesus movement in the context of Jewish
Palestinian society. In Hellenistic society, by contrast, it was
given a positive welcome. A sociological theory of conflict is an
inadequate explanation of this. For in comparison with other eras
of world history, the Roman empire during the first two centuries
of the Christian era was one of those rare exceptions, a period
characterized by peace and stability, prosperity and open com-
munications. The Hellenistic cities on the Mediterranean flourished and reached new peaks of civilization, only to be regained in
modern times. Of course there were tensions, but it seems more
appropriate to consider them in terms of the way in which society
integrated them and balanced them out. Consequently a sociological theory of integration is a more appropriate perspec-

tive from which to approach an analysis of earliest Hellenistic Christianity and from which to assess and co-ordinate the relevant sociological data (which here too are very sparse). The basic question is: how were relatively stable and sturdy communities with considerable inner cohesion formed from a mixture of ethnic, social and religious groups? How did Jews and Gentiles, Greeks and barbarians, slaves and freemen, men and women, come to form a new unity in Christ (cf. Gal. 3.28; I Cor. 12.13; Rom. 1.14)?

The transition from the Jesus movement in Palestine to the earliest Hellenistic Christianity is bound up with a deep-seated change in role-structure. Whereas in earliest Palestinian Christianity the wandering charismatics were the decisive authorities, in a Hellenistic setting the chief emphasis was soon laid on local communities: the resident authorities to be found in them soon became the normative figures for earliest Christianity, first of all as a collegiate body, and then as early as the beginning of the second century as a monarchical episcopate (Ignatius of Antioch). On the other hand, the successors of the earliest Christian wandering charismatics were increasingly brought into disrepute, as is shown by III John. One consequence of this change in structure is that the early Christian literature which came into being in the Hellenistic communities (above all the corpus of epistles in the New Testament) is primarily oriented on interactions within the local community as far as ethical instructions are concerned. This is also true of the letters written by the wandering preacher Paul. The radical ethics of the synoptic tradition is only handed down with reservations. Paul hardly ever cites words of Jesus. And even if he had known a number of them, the ethnic radicalism of the Jesus movement, its pattern of dispensing with family, homeland, possessions and protection, would hardly have found a place in the communities which he founded. Rather, within these communities there arose a more moderate patriarchalism of love, oriented on the need for social interaction within the Christian community – on the problems of the common life of masters and slaves, men and women, parents and children (cf. Col. 3.18ff.; Eph. 5.22ff.). The restructuring of roles even extended to that of the revealer. Whereas the Son of man christology is governed by a movement in the ascendant (the one who is now despised and persecuted will become the judge of the world), the Hellenistic communities added a movement in the opposite direction: the pre-existent Son of God empties himself and humiliates himself in our world. Paul can connect this development with the social structures of the earliest Christian communities not only metaphorically, but also as a matter of fact. The humiliation of the Son of God is voluntary impoverishment: 'For you know the grace of our Lord Jesus Christ, that though he was rich, yet for your sake he became poor' (II Cor. 8.9). His manifestation in such a ridiculous fashion corresponded with the fact that most of the members of Christian communities came from the lower classes (I Cor. 1.26ff.). Here too, then, we can establish a structural homologue between the earliest Christian groups and the role of the revealer.

In the same way, an analysis of the factors in earliest Hellenistic Christianity points to far-reaching changes. Here we must content ourselves with a brief sketch of the most important factors:

(*a*) There was a fundamental change in the socio-economic situation. Although the Hellenistic communities may not have amassed great riches, they were still in a position to support the Palestinian communities (Gal. 2.10; Rom. 15.15ff.; I Cor 16.1ff.; II Cor. 8f.; Acts 11.27ff.). The place of wandering charismatics with no social roots was taken to an increasing extent by Christians with a high position in society; true, in Corinth these formed only a small minority (I Cor. 1.26ff.), but as almost all the members of the congregation whom Paul names can be reckoned as being among the upper classes (as far as we learn anything about their social status), we may conclude that the Christians who counted in a community belonged to the more privileged classes.[38] Pliny the Younger explicitly confirms that people of every class (*omnis ordinis*) were Christians (*Ep.* X. 96.9). An attempt at an effective compensation[39] between classes increasingly took the place of a rigorous criticism of property and riches. The situation in the Shepherd of Hermas seems to be that the rich supported the poor with their possessions and the poor the rich with their prayers. For the rich man is poor in his relationship to God, and the poor man is rich in faith (*Similitudes* II.5ff.).

(*b*) Socio-ecological changes are no less decisive. A movement which was formerly connected with the country became a group based on the cities. When Pliny the Younger writes that Christianity spread 'not only through the cities, but also through the villages and the countryside' (*Ep.* X 96.9), it is clear where Christianity has its focal point. Developing cities with their new increase in population were more open to the new message than the country, with its traditionalist attitudes. Groups of this kind in particular, whose roots in the cities were not too deep, could find security and support in the communities. It is probably a consequence of the change from country to city that the vivid concrete pictures of the synoptic tradition increasingly give place to abstract argumentation: primitive Christian literature becomes more theological, more speculative, more reflective.

(*c*) The situation in Hellenistic civilization differed from that in Palestine in socio-political terms. Palestine was a powder barrel within which the Mediterranean cities kept the tensions within bounds. Earliest Hellenistic Christianity was largely in accord with the political structures of its environment, though always with the eschatological proviso that this whole world would in any case soon pass away. Paul, for example, is well integrated into Hellenistic society in this respect. He was both a citizen of the city state of Tarsus in Asia Minor (Acts 21.39) and a Roman citizen (Acts 22.25ff.). Radical theocratic ideas were quite alien to him. He seldom used the concept of the kingdom of God, and indeed it retreated well into the background in the earliest Hellenistic Christianity. It drew its strength from the socio-political tensions of Palestine and dissatisfaction with the existing structures of government. Paul is far removed from such dissatisfaction. For him all authorities are from God (Rom. 13.1ff.).

(*d*) The change from Palestine to the Hellenistic world was bound up with a far-reaching socio-cultural change. Primitive Christianity extended into an area where a new language was spoken. It had to come to grips with philosophical schools and compete with other religions. It was confronted with a wealth of new traditions, norms and values. Only now did it enter the 'wider' world. Only now were its writings addressed to a larger public, for example in the apologies written in the second century. Only now did it become an independent religion. For originally it had been a renewal movement within Judaism, an origin to which it owes a rich heritage: monotheism, a lofty ethic, the acuteness of prophetic criticism, a universalistic view of history – in short, the Old Testament and its great figures. With all this, however, it also took over the ethnocentricity of the Jewish people which it continually transformed by representing itself as the 'true Israel' and associating with this view a claim to absoluteness which was no longer restricted or toned down by ethnic boundaries. It emerged with this claim to absoluteness in a Gentile world which was characterized by a relatively great degree of religious tolerance; it put in question the foundations of a world from whose tolerance it benefited at the same time.

If we take all the factors into account, we can understand why the Hellenistic world was more favourable than that of Palestine for earliest Christianity: the vision of love and reconciliation may have been born in a society rent by crises, but it had no chances of realization here. The new vision was more in accord with the less tense world of the Hellenistic cities (here too there were considerable tensions between city and country: the cities were privileged). Here there was a considerable degree of local and social mobility, an urge for communication between very different groups of people and a need for integration. Here an eirenic movement had more chance from the start. In the relatively peaceful period down to the beginning of the third century AD it succeeded in building up a stable organization and establishing institutional norms like a pattern of ministry, a canon and a confession of faith. It succeeded in creating a social balance between the different classes within society and in differentiating itself from radical tendencies like Montanism and Gnosticism, so that despite massive persecutions it was able to survive the great political, social and economic crisis which shattered the Roman empire in the third century AD, whereas the traditional political and religious institutions emerged from it weakened. When he reorganized the empire, Constantine could rely on a small, well-organized Christian minority, which had proved itself in critical situations, to give the state internal support at a time of increasing social pressure. Christianity became more and more the social cement of the totalitarian state of late antiquity. The vision of love and reconciliation faded. But it still continued to flicker. Some 'fools in Christ' pursued it, who tended to be classified as religious 'virtuosi', so that they did not have to be taken too seriously. Yet it could be that the pattern of love of one's enemy, of renunciation of power and freedom towards possessions, which are thought by many to be the 'Sunday norms' of world history, are also significant for everyday life at a time when our social relationships are becoming increasingly fluid. The necessity for inward and outward peace, coupled with the urgency of social change, perhaps requires of us more of a radical change in attitudes than we realize. What has failed to function so far may one day prove to be functional, and what has been counted as an ethical luxury may prove to be mankind's chance of survival.[40]

Notes

1. There is hardly any literature which gives a thematic treatment of the sociology of earliest Palestinian Christianity. The studies which are predominantly inspired by Marxism often make only selective use of historical-critical scholarship, though they contain valuable suggestions: see K. Kautsky, *Der Ursprung des Christentums*, Stuttgart [11]1921; P. Alfaric, *Die sozialen Ursprünge des Christentums*, Darmstadt 1963; M. Robbe, *Der Ursprung des Christentums*, Leipzig 1967. The following theological studies may be mentioned: R. Schumacher, *Die soziale Lage der Christen im apostolischen Zeitalter*, Paderborn 1924; S. J. Case, *The Social Origins of Christianity*, Chicago 1923; E. Lohmeyer, *Soziale Fragen im Urchristentum* 1921 = Darmstadt 1973; F. C. Grant, *The Economic Background of the Gospels*, Oxford 1926; P. Seidensticker, 'Die Gemeinschaftsformen der religiösen Gruppen des Spätjudentums und der Urkirche', *Stud. Bibl. Franc.* IX, Jerusalem 1959, 94–198; G. Baumbach, *Jesus von Nazareth im Lichte der jüdischen Gruppenbildung*, Berlin 1971; M. Hengel, *Property and Riches in the Early Church*, ET London and Philadelphia 1974. Many good sociological comments can be found – often made in passing – in studies of the historical Jesus, of early ecclesiology, of social ethics and above all of contemporary history. Two basic works which have contributed to the introduction of sociological perspectives need to be mentioned here: J. Jeremias, *Jerusalem in the Time of Jesus*, ET London and Philadelphia 1969; M. Hengel, *Judaism and Hellenism*, ET London and Philadelphia 1974.

2. See my remarks in 'Theoretische Probleme religionssoziologischer Forschung und die Analyse des Urchristentums', *NZSysTR* 16, 1974, 35–56.

3. See also my article 'Die soziologische Auswertung religiöser Überlieferungen', *Kairos* 17, 1975, 284–99.

4. We can note both a large-scale and a small-scale sociological continuity. There were no fundamental changes within Palestinian Jewish society as a whole between the ministry of Jesus (*c*.AD 25–30) and the Jesus movement after Easter (*c*.AD 30–70). What was possible from a

sociological point of view in AD 30–70 was also possible in the previous five years. Small-scale continuity is rather more questionable. It is indisputable that this continuity existed on the personal level (the group of disciples from the period before Easter handed on the faith after Easter); it is also the case that the disciples continued their mode of life as travelling preachers. In this way they continued the activity of Jesus as a wandering charismatic. Where form-critical scepticism about the historicity of our traditions is based on the assumption of a sociological rift between the wandering preachers of Jesus and the settled local communities, its grounding is inadequate.

5. Jacob Burckhardt, *Griechische Kulturgeschichte*, Gesammelte Werke 5, Berlin [1955], 6.

6. This transference of the theory of roles to subjects of religious belief is supported by H. Sundén, *Die Religion und die Rollen*, Berlin 1966; id., *Gott erfahren. Das Rollenangebot der Religionen*, GTB 98, Gütersloh 1975. For the role of the wandering charismatic cf. G. Kretschmar, 'Ein Beitrag zur Frage nach dem Ursprung frühchristlicher Askese', *ZTK* 61, 1964, 27–67; M. Hengel, *Nachfolge und Charisma*, BZNW 34, Berlin 1968; G. Theissen, 'Wanderradikalismus', *ZTK* 70, 1973, 245–71.

7. See the extremely interesting analysis of the Sermon on the Mount in D. v. Oppen, *Die personale Gesellschaft*, GTB 39, Gütersloh 1967, 9ff.

8. 'Structural homologues' between social reality and spiritual manifestations are made the favourite object of research in 'genetic structuralism', in the context of the sociology of literature; cf. L. Goldmann, 'Die Soziologie der Literatur', *Literatursoziologie* I, ed. J. Bark, Stuttgart 1974, 85–113.

9. This is the thesis of O. Plöger in *Theocracy and Eschatology*, ET Oxford 1968.

10. A. Schlatter, *Neutestamentliche Theologie* I, Calw/Stuttgart 1909, 10, postulated a unity of thought and action which is also true of sociological investigations.

11. I have presented the following ideas at length in '"Wir haben alles verlassen" (Mk 10, 28). Nachfolge und soziale Entwurzelung in der jüdisch-palästinischen Gesellschaft des 1. Jahrhunderts n.Chr.', *NovTest* 19, 1977, 161–96.

12. Gospel of the Nazaraeans, frag. 33 (E. Hennecke and W. Schneemelcher, *New Testament Apocrypha* I, ET ed. R. McL. Wilson, 2nd imp. London 1973, p. 152).

13. For robbers and resistance fighters see the fundamental work by M. Hengel, *Die Zeloten. Untersuchungen zur jüdischen Freiheitsbewegung in der Zeit von Herodes I. bis 70 n.Chr.*, Leiden/Köln ²1976.

14. For 'lack of principle' cf. H. Braun, *Spätjüdisch-häretischer und frühchristlicher Radikalismus*, BHT 24, Tübingen 1957, 7ff.

15. Thus G. Baumbach, 'Zeloten und Sikarier', *TLZ* 90, 1965, 727–40, col. 731.

16. For the economic situation in Palestine in the first century AD cf. above all J. Klausner, *Jesus of Nazareth*, ET London and New York 1925, pp. 174–93; F. C. Grant (see n.1 above); J. Jeremias (see n.1); F. M. Heichelheim, 'Roman Syria', in T. Frank (ed.), *An Economic Survey of Ancient Rome* IV, Baltimore 1938, 121–257; H. Kreissig, *Die sozialen Zusammenhänge des jüdischen Krieges*, Berlin 1970.

17. B. Colomb and Y. Kedar, 'Ancient Agriculture in the Galilee Mountains', *IEJ* 21, 1971, 136–40.

18. There is an interpretation of the history of Jewish religion in terms of conflict between city and country in L. Finkelstein, *The Pharisees: The Sociological Backgrounds of their Faith*, Philadelphia 1938. M. Rostovtzeff, *The Social and Economic History of the Roman Empire*, Oxford [2]1957, has stressed the significance of the conflict between city and country for the whole of ancient social history. I have made an attempt to interpret aspects of the ministry of Jesus in terms of this conflict in 'Die Tempelweissagung Jesu. Prophetie im Spannungsfeld von Stadt und Land', *TZ* 32, 1976, 144–58.

19. Cf. N. Brockmeyer, *Arbeitsorganisation und ökonomisches Denken in der Gutswirtschaft des römischen Reiches*, Bochum dissertation 1968. For Palestine in particular see M. Hengel, 'Das Gleichnis von den Weingärtnern Mc 12, 1–12 im Lichte der Zenonpapyri und der rabbinischen Gleichnisse', *ZNW* 59, 1968, 1–39. For absenteeism see op. cit., 21f.

20. For this group see M. Hengel, 'Zwischen Jesus und Paulus. Die "Hellenisten", die "Sieben" und Stephanus', *ZTK* 72, 1975, 151–206.

21. For the political history of Palestine see E. Schürer, *A History of the Jewish People in the Age of Jesus Christ*, Vol. 1, ET, rev. ed., Edinburgh 1973; S. Safrai and M. Stern (eds.), *The Jewish People in the First Century*, Compendium Rerum Iudaicarum ad NT I, 1, Assen 1974.

22. Cf. A. H. M. Jones, 'The Urbanization of Palestine', *JRS* 21, 1931, 78–85; id., *The Cities of the Eastern Roman Provinces*, Oxford 1937, 227–95; A. Alt, 'Hellenistische Städte und Domänen in Galiläa', in *Kleine Schriften* 2, Munich 1953, 384–95; E. A. Judge, *Christliche Gruppen in nichtchristlicher Gessellschaft*, Wuppertal 1974, 12ff.

23. For this reform attempt cf. E. Bickermann, *Der Gott der Makkabäer*, Berlin 1937; M. Hengel, *Judaism and Hellenism* I, ET London and Philadelphia 1974, 267ff.

24. The term *ecclesia* was handed down through Hellenistic Judaism,

cf. K. Berger, 'Volksversammlung und Gemeinde Gottes', *ZTK* 73, 1976, 167–207.

25. For the politics of the high priests cf. G. Baumbach, *Jesus von Nazareth* (see n.1), 49–71; E. M. Smallwood, 'High Priests and Politics in Roman Palestine', *JTS* 13, 1962, 14–34.

26. For the Sadducees and Pharisees cf. J. Wellhausen, *Die Pharisäer und Sadduzäer*, Göttingen ³1967; M. Weber, 'Die Pharisäer', in *Gesammelte Aufsätze zur Religionssoziologie* 3, Tübingen 1923, 401–42; H. Kreissig, 'Zur Rolle der religiösen Gruppen in den Volksbewegungen der Hasmonäerzeit', *Klio* 43, 1965, 174–82; R. Meyer, *Tradition und Neuschöpfung im antiken Judentum*, Leipzig 1965; J. Neusner, *From Politics to Piety. The Emergence of Pharisaic Judaism*, Englewood Cliffs 1973.

27. For the Herods see A. Schalit, *König Herodes*, Berlin 1969; H. W. Hoehner, *Herod Antipas*, Cambridge 1972; S. Perowne, *The Later Herods*, London 1958.

28. Cf. W. R. Farmer, Judas, Simon and Athronges', *NTS* 4, 1958, 147–55.

29. For the phenomenon of the stricter interpretation of the Torah in Judaism see H. Braun, *Spätjüdisch-häretischer und frühchristlicher Radikalismus*. For connections between Hellenism and ethical proclamation in the Jesus movement cf. H. Hommel, 'Herrenworte im Lichte sokratischer Überlieferung', *ZNW* 57, 1966, 1–23. The enormously learned work by K. Berger, *Die Gesetzesauslegung Jesu*, WMANT 40, Neukirchen 1972, is a real treasure house. However, in my view the connections and analogies which he brings out and substantiates need not necessarily be interpreted in this way: in its interpretation of the law the Jesus movement did not just continue existing traditions. Analogies between Hellenistic Judaism and the Jesus movement may be derived from the fact that they existed in comparable situations: the Jesus movement, too, gave an answer to problems which Judaism faced over the advance of Hellenism.

30. For the cultural encounter of Hellenism and Judaism cf. M. Hengel, *Judaism and Hellenism*; id., *Juden, Griechen und Barbaren*, SBS 76, Stuttgart 1976.

31. For individual philosophers see the relevant sections of K. Praechter, *Die Philosophie des Altertums*, Basel/Stuttgart 1967.

32. S. W. Baron, *A Social and Religious History of the Jews* I, New York 1952, 188–95, gives a survey of antisemitism in antiquity.

33. T. Ling, *A History of Religion East and West*, London 1968, 212.

34. Here I follow ideas on the social conditioning of art and literature which are summarized in T. W. Adorno's posthumous work *Ästhetische*

Theorie, Frankfurt 1970. On the other hand, the concept of the 'functional autonomy of motives' comes from the psychologist G. H. Allport, 'Entstehung und Umgestaltung der Motive', in *Die Motivation menschlichen Handelns*, ed. H. Thomae, Köln 1965, 488–97.

35. The following section makes use of psycho-analytic terminology in its analysis. For the problem of a psycho-analytic hermeneutics cf. Y. Spiegel (ed.), *Psychoanalytische Interpretationen biblischer Texte*, Munich 1972. At first sight, much of the interpretation collected there will seem utterly chaotic to the historical-critical exegete. Nevertheless, it does seem to me that there are stimuli for further criticism. I intend to comment on this elsewhere. However, to avoid at least some misunderstandings I shall make a few points here: (1) The focal point of the following considerations consists in ego-functions (the so-called defence mechanisms of the ego) and not the motive force of the id. (2) It is assumed that biblical symbols represent and give form to psychodynamic processes and do not simply obscure them. (3) No account is taken of aggressive drives. All aggression is mediated socially by frustration and organically through human anxiety-reactions; cf. R. Denker, *Angst und Aggression*, Stuttgart 1974.

36. Cf. the illuminating observations on primitive Christian exorcisms by W. E. Mühlmann, *Chiliasmus und Nativismus*, Berlin 1961, 252. He points out that in Siberia, oppression by an alien people is sometimes depicted as possession by an alien demon.

37. Cf. P. Berger, *The Social Reality of Religion*, London 1969 (= *The Sacred Canopy*, New York 1969), pp. 73–80. Berger sees a close 'relationship between Biblical theology and the masochistic attitude' (p. 73) – even in christology. By masochism he understands the introjection of aggression: the question of the justification of God in view of earthly suffering is replaced with the question of man's sinfulness (Job) and the sinful man is justified by the suffering God (Christ). However, the intention of New Testament christology is not the sublime enjoyment of one's own suffering and one's own guilt (that would be masochism), but liberation from suffering and guilt. The aim of the christological imagery is in fact to replace aggressive impulses – even the introjected aggression of an awareness of guilt – with love and reconciliation (even within oneself). Without doubt, however, the glorification of a sublime masochism is one of the great dangers of Christianity.

39. I have attempted to shed light on social conditions in the Corinthian community in a number of articles: 'Soziale Schichtung in der korinthischen Gemeinde', *ZNW* 65, 1974, 232–72; id., 'Soziale Integration und sakramentalesHandeln', *NovTest* 24, 1974, 179–206; 'Die Starken und Schwachen in Korinth', *EvTh* 35, 1975, 155–72; 'Legitimät und Lebensunterhalt', *NTS* 21, 1975, 192–221.

39. M. Hengel has coined the impressive formula 'The Compromise of Effective Compensation' for the social ethos of primitive Christianity in the second century AD, cf. *Property and Riches* (see n.1 above), pp. 60ff.

40. A good deal more could be said, for example, on the consequences of a sociology of the Jesus movement for the quest of the historical Jesus, for christology, ethics, church practice. I hope some time to be able to present my thoughts on fundamental theological questions elsewhere. I must therefore limit myself to a few remarks which I wish were unnecessary. (1) Anyone who thinks that a sociology of the Jesus movement is a rewarding undertaking is not therefore aspiring to a theology of social structures or a sociological theology or a theological sociology or anything of that kind. (2) Anyone who learns from Marxism and finds it stimulating as a result to apply theories of conflicts in society to the interpretation of social and religious processes is not necessarily a Marxist. Remember Rolf Dahrendorf! (3) Anyone who writes about the radicalism of the early Christian wandering charismatics and finds it difficult to deny his sympathies for them is still some way from being a radical.

Index of References

1. Biblical references

2. Other authors and works